A CLASSIC RETELLING

Julius Caesar

by William Shakespeare

nextext

Cover photograph: Bryan Reinhart/Masterfile

Printed in the United States of America.

ISBN 0-618-03148-0

1 2 3 4 5 6 7 — QKT — 06 05 04 03 02 01 00

Picture Acknowledgements

Pages 10, 16–17, 18–19, 26: North Wind Picture Archives

Page 15: The Granger Collection

Page 20: CORBIS/Chris Heller

Pages 12, 23: from *The Complete Works of Shakespeare,* edited by David Bevington. Copyright © 1997 by Addison-Wesley Educational Publishers Inc. Reprinted by permission.

Page 25: The British Library

Table of Contents

Background 10

The Story of *Julius Caesar*

Shakespeare's Theater

Shakespeare's Language

The Characters

The Plot

Shakespeare's Life

A Shakespeare Time Line

ACT ONE

Scene One 28

On a street in Rome on February 15th, 44 B.C., a large crowd is celebrating Julius Caesar's victory over his enemy, Pompey. Flavius and Marullus, two government officials who supported Pompey, are angry. Marullus reminds the crowd that they used to like Pompey. The crowd leaves, and the two men take down the decorations honoring Caesar.

Scene Two 33

In Rome, Caesar brings his wife Calpurnia to the race on the feast of Lupercal. In the crowd is a person who warns Caesar to beware the Ides

of March (March 15). Cassius tries to turn Brutus against Caesar. Casca tells them that Antony has offered Caesar a crown three times, but Caesar refused it each time. He also reports that Flavius and Marullus lost their jobs for taking down the decorations. Brutus and Cassius agree to meet the next day. Cassius plans to leave fake letters for Brutus suggesting that the Romans want him to stop Caesar.

Scene Three **49**

On March 14, there is a violent thunderstorm. Casca fears that the storm and other things predict terrible events to come. Cassius says Caesar is the cause and persuades Casca to join with others to stop Caesar. Cassius tells Cinna to put the fake letters where Brutus will find them. Cassius and Casca plan to visit Brutus later that night and talk him into joining them. If Brutus is on their side, people will think they are honorable.

ACT TWO

Scene One **58**

Before dawn on the Ides of March, Brutus can't sleep. He is worrying that Caesar may become king. Brutus's ancestor helped begin the Republic. Must he now kill Caesar to save the Republic? His servant brings him one of Cassius's letters.

Cassius and his followers arrive. They talk about their plans. Cassius thinks Mark Antony should be killed as well. Brutus disagrees. After everyone leaves, Brutus's wife Portia enters. She wants to know why he is worried. He says he will tell her later and leaves to go to the Capitol.

Scene Two **75**

At his house, Caesar gets ready to go to the Capitol. Calpurnia thinks the strange signs she sees mean that Caesar will be harmed. She begs him to stay home. The priests, too, advise Caesar to stay home. He agrees. Then, after Decius Brutus arrives, Caesar decides he will not lie and say he is sick. Decius flatters Caesar and tells him that the Senate will crown him today. His enemies arrive, and so does Mark Antony. Caesar believes he is among friends.

Scene Three **83**

On a street near the Capitol, Artemidorus reads his note warning Caesar about the plot. He plans to pass the note to Caesar as he goes by.

Scene Four **85**

In front of Brutus's house, Portia sends Lucius to the Capitol to find out what's happening. She talks to a person who plans to warn Caesar. He is a soothsayer, someone who claims to see the future. Portia worries about Brutus's part in the plot.

ACT THREE

Scene One **90**

Outside the Capitol, the soothsayer and Artemidorus try to warn Caesar. Caesar goes into the Capitol. His enemies surround him, pretending to plead for Metellus Cimber's brother. Suddenly, they rush Caesar and stab him to death. Mark Antony flees. Brutus persuades the murderers not to hurt Mark Antony. He says that he will explain the killing to the Roman people and that Antony should speak at Caesar's funeral. When Antony is left alone with Caesar's dead body, he vows revenge.

Scene Two **106**

In the Forum, Brutus speaks to the people about why Caesar's ambition was dangerous to Rome. The people cheer Brutus and want him to take Caesar's place. Then Antony speaks. He asks why, if Caesar was ambitious, he refused the crown three times. Antony wins the people to his side by reading Caesar's will, in which he leaves his wealth to the people. Antony calls Caesar's murderers "honorable men," but he encourages the people to hate them. The crowd rushes off to kill the murderers. Octavius has arrived in Rome, but Brutus and Cassius have fled.

ACT FOUR

kills himself. Brutus arrives from defeating Octavius's army. He mourns the deaths and prepares to attack again.

Scene Four **167**
In another part of the battlefield, Brutus and his army are in trouble. Lucilius, who pretends to be Brutus, is taken prisoner and brought to Antony. He tells Antony that Brutus will never be taken alive.

Scene Five **170**
In another part of the field, Brutus kills himself to avoid being captured. Antony and Octavius honor Brutus and the battle ends.

Vocabulary words appear in boldface type and are footnoted. Specialized or technical words and phrases appear in lightface type and are footnoted.

Background

William Shakespeare lived and wrote near the end of a time in European history known as the Renaissance, which lasted from 1485 to 1660. (Both the voyages of Christopher Columbus and the Pilgrims' landing at Plymouth happened during the Renaissance.) The word *renaissance* means "rebirth." During this time, there was a rebirth of interest in the arts and sciences of the classical Greeks and Romans of 350 B.C. to 500 A.D. Shakespeare took the plot of *Julius Caesar* from the writings of the ancient Greek historian Plutarch. In fact, some of the story is line for line as he found it in a translation by Sir Thomas North. Both Plutarch and Shakespeare slightly changed the facts to make the story more exciting.

The Story of *Julius Caesar*

Julius Caesar was a Roman general and politician who lived from about 100 to 44 B.C. One of the greatest military leaders in Roman history, Caesar conquered most of Gaul (now France) and began the invasion of Britain. His victories brought Roman ways to Europe and also made him very popular at home.

Caesar gained so much military power that Pompey (a general who was a ruler in Rome) and the Roman Senate feared he would try to control the government. To keep that from happening, the Senate ordered him back to Rome. He disobeyed and instead led his army in a civil war. Caesar's army quickly took Rome, and Pompey and his friends fled.

Caesar's armies went on to defeat Pompey in Greece, Asia, Spain, and Egypt. In 46 B.C., he returned to Rome a hero. The Senate appointed him dictator. In 44 B.C., he was named dictator for life.

Then, on March 15, a day known as the Ides of March, a group of senators murdered Caesar in the senate.

◀ Caesar orders his troops to cross the Rubicon River. This action led to the civil war that ended with his becoming dictator.

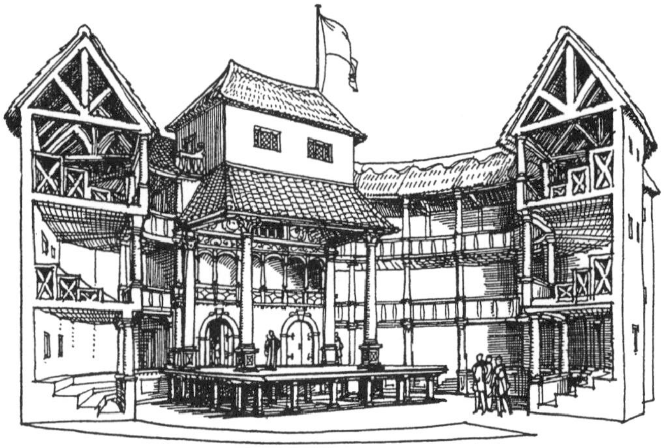

▲
Theater of Shakespeare's time

Shakespeare's Theater

The Globe theater was built in 1599 in a small town outside London called Southwark. It was an outdoor summer theater. In 1613, the theater burned down. It was rebuilt in 1614 but was torn down in 1644. However, in London today, Shakespeare's plays are performed in a newly built Globe theater. Now, as in the old times, when the flag is flying over the Globe, a play is going on.

The Globe theater was round and had no roof. The stage stuck out into the audience. As many as 2,000 people attended the plays. Most of them stood on the ground around the stage. There were three covered balconies for the audience. The most expensive seats were on the shady side.

The stage had doors on either side. There was a small curtain-covered room at the back of the stage and two balconies above it. The first balcony could have been used to show action inside Caesar's house while the stage would show the street outside. The second balcony was for the musicians whose music was like a sound track for the play. Above the stage was a ceiling painted to look like the sky. It was held up by two columns. Above the ceiling was a special-effects room. There cannons were fired for the battle scenes. (One of these cannons set off the fire in 1613.) The stage also had a trap door that could be used for magical appearances.

In the play you will find stage directions, for example [*They fight.*]. These tell the actors what to do.

There were no lights in the theater. Plays were presented during the day. There was no scenery, except perhaps for a table or chair. Scene changes were very fast and there were beautiful and expensive costumes.

Shakespeare's Language

Poetry

Shakespeare wrote his plays in verse. Some of it does not rhyme and some of it does. The meter, or rhythm of the language, is what makes it poetry. Shakespeare's poetry is in ten-syllable lines with alternating stresses. This kind of verse is called "iambic pentameter." For example:

Farewell, good Strato—Caesar, now be still!
I killed not thee with half so good a will.

In the retelling given here, poetry is not used. However, some of Shakespeare's most famous lines have been included. A note will tell you when three or more lines are exactly as Shakespeare wrote them.

Imagery

In Act One, Scene Three, Casca talks about the thunderstorm. He says, "Are you not upset when the earth shakes? O Cicero, I have seen storms when the howling winds have broken mighty oak trees, and I have seen the ocean rage and foam, trying to reach the sky. But never until tonight, never until now, did I see a storm raining fire. There must be war in heaven, or else the gods think the world is too evil and are trying to destroy it."

This language gives the audience powerful images of the storm. Shakespeare makes great use of imagery throughout his plays.

Puns and Other Fun with Words

Shakespeare loved to have fun with language. He enjoyed jokes. He liked phrases that have more than one meaning. His writing shows off the many meanings that can be made from a single statement. In the opening scene of *Julius Caesar,* a shoemaker mocks a government official by answering his questions in riddles. When asked what work he does, he says, "I mend bad soles." The shoemaker's speech gives several examples of Shakespeare's fun with words. There are many others throughout the play.

▲
The Soothsayer warns Caesar.

The Characters

▲
Julius Caesar

Caesar's Party

Julius Caesar—the dictator of Rome

Calpurnia—Caesar's wife

Octavius Caesar—Caesar's adopted son and heir; one of the three generals (the Triumvirate) who take control of Rome after Julius Caesar's death

Mark Antony—Caesar's favorite general; a member of the Triumvirate

Marcus Lepidus—the third and least important member of the Triumvirate

Soothsayer—an old man who can see the future

Artemidorus—a teacher who has a note for Caesar

Ghost—the ghost of Caesar

His Enemies' Party

Cassius—a Roman general; organizer of the group who kill Julius Caesar

Marcus Brutus—Cassius's brother-in-law; becomes leader of the group against Caesar

Portia—Brutus's wife; daughter of an enemy of Caesar

Flavius and Marullus—Tribunes (government officials)

Casca

Others Against Caesar

Trebonius
Ligarius
Decius Brutus
Metellus Cimber
Cinna

Background Caesar's enemies murder him at the capitol.

Brutus's and Cassius's Friends Who Support Them in the War

- **Lucilius**
- **Titinius**
- **Messala**
- **Young Cato**
- **Volumnius**

Brutus's Servants

- **Varro**
- **Clitus**
- **Claudius**
- **Strato**
- **Lucius**
- **Dardanius**

Cassius's Servant

- **Pindarus**

Senators

Cicero—a famous speaker and leader of the Senate

Publius

Popilius Lena

Poets

Cinna—a poet in Rome who unluckily has the same name as one of the conspirators

Another Poet

Others

- **Senators**
- **Citizens**
- **Guards**
- **Soldiers**
- **Messengers**
- **Plebeians**

The Plot

Act Three

Caesar is murdered.

Climax

Act Two

Brutus joins the group. Despite warnings, Caesar goes to the Senate.

Rising Action

Act One

A group plans to kill Julius Caesar. They believe he wants to become king.

Beginning

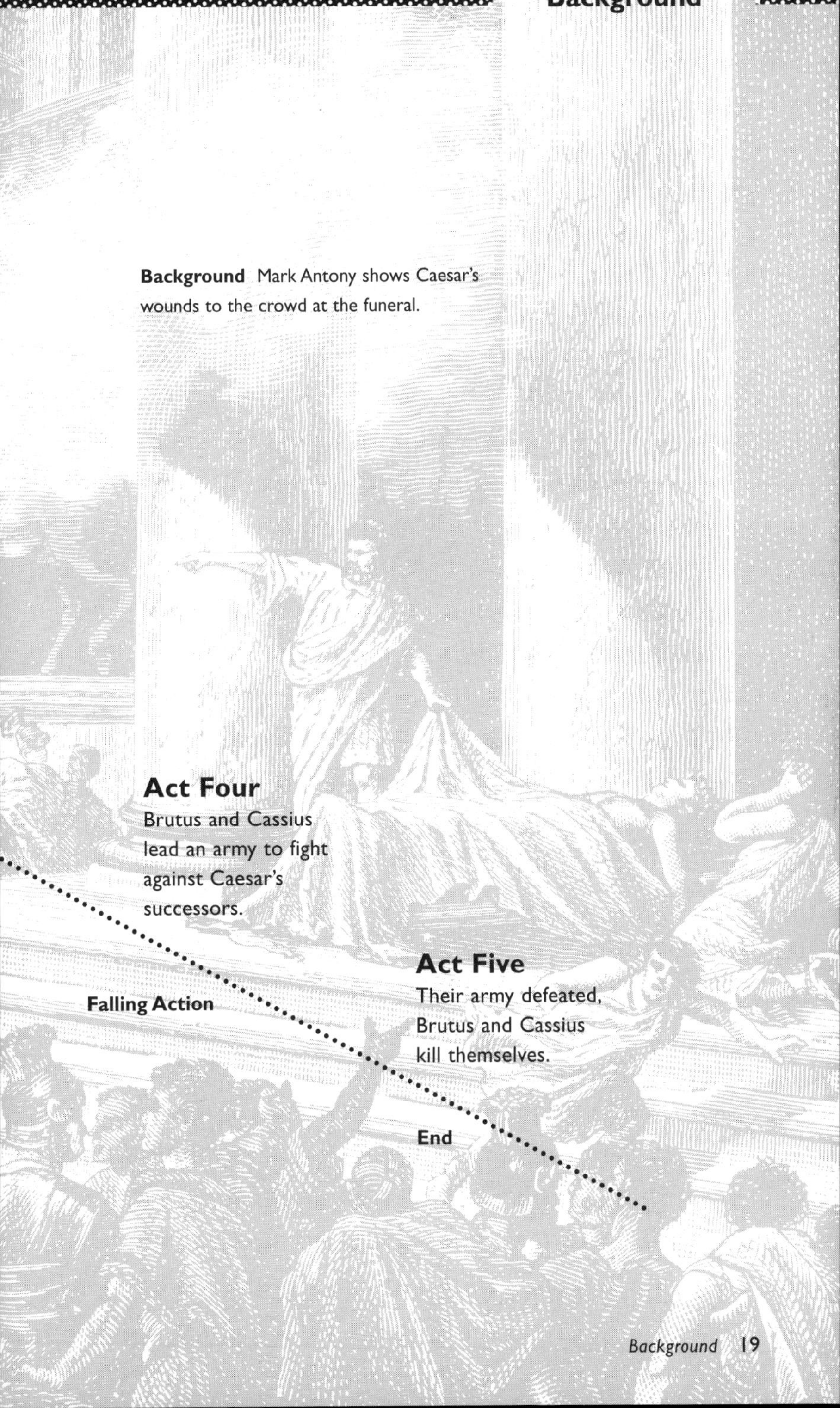

Background Mark Antony shows Caesar's wounds to the crowd at the funeral.

Act Four

Brutus and Cassius lead an army to fight against Caesar's successors.

Falling Action

Act Five

Their army defeated, Brutus and Cassius kill themselves.

End

▲
William Shakespeare

Shakespeare's Life

Birth

Shakespeare was born in Stratford-upon-Avon, a small town about seventy-five miles northwest of London, England. His father, John Shakespeare, was a glove maker who owned a shop in Stratford and was elected to local government offices. Shakespeare's mother, Mary Arden, came from a farming family. Shakespeare was baptized on April 26, 1564, a few days after his birth. He was the third of eight children.

Childhood

Shakespeare went to school in Stratford. At this time, most people did not get an education and could neither read nor write. His school day was nine hours long. Shakespeare's education gave him the background for much of his writing. At school, he may have first read Plutarch's *Lives of the Noble Greeks and Romans,* on which *Julius Caesar* is based.

Stratford was an excellent place to grow up. The town was surrounded by woods, fields, and farms. It was a market town where people came to buy and sell goods. It was very busy, and Shakespeare had a chance to meet and observe many different types of people. During holidays,

▲
Stratford

popular plays were performed. Traveling companies of actors visited the town, and there were two large fairs every year.

Marriage

In November 1582, at the age of eighteen, Shakespeare married Anne Hathaway, who was twenty-six. Their daughter Susanna was born in May 1583. Twins, Hamnet, a boy, and Judith, a girl, were born in 1585.

Queen Elizabeth I ▶

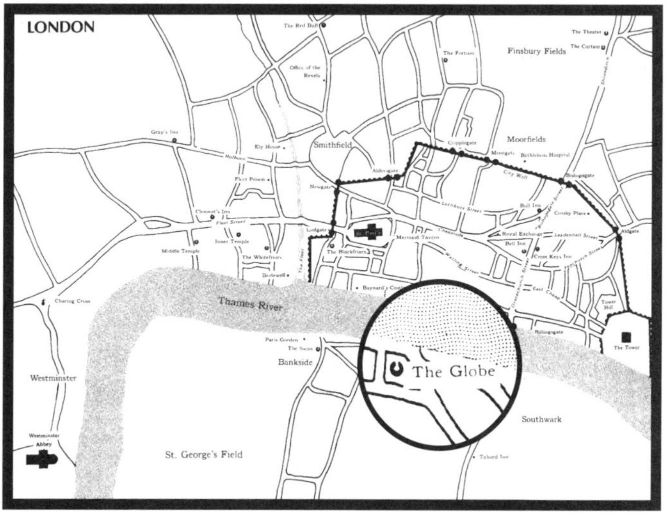

▲
Map of London

London

Seven years after the twins were born, Shakespeare was in London. He worked in the theaters—first in small jobs, then as an actor, and finally as a writer of plays. In 1599, he and six others became owners of the new Globe theater. Queen Elizabeth I supported Shakespeare's company. James I, who became king in 1603, also gave money to Shakespeare's theater company. After that, it was known as the King's Men and often presented plays for the royal court.

Writing

Shakespeare's first plays were like those of another very popular author, Christopher Marlowe. As Shakespeare wrote more, he developed his own style. He wrote thirty-seven plays in all. His success came in part because he knew firsthand how audiences behaved and what they wanted. He gave audiences exciting stories. He provided funny moments in tragedies and tragic moments in the middle of comedies. He knew how easily audiences got bored and restless. He made sure there were surprises, magic events, songs, fights, love scenes, and jokes in all his plays.

The years 1592 to 1594 were times of great sickness and disease. The bubonic plague hit London, and the theaters were often closed. Then Shakespeare turned to writing poems. He wrote two, long, story-telling poems based on Greek mythology, *Venus and Adonis* (1593) and *The Rape of Lucrece* (1594). He also wrote a collection of 154 of the fourteen-line poems known as sonnets.

Later Years

Shakespeare's work brought him fame and money. In 1597, he bought himself a very large house called New Place in Stratford. He moved into it and spent more and more of his time there. His last play was *The Tempest.* In it, a magician who has lived on a deserted magical island returns to his own land after he breaks his magical staff. Shakespeare seems to have gone on helping to write and fix other people's plays after he stopped writing his own. He died in 1616 and was buried in the church at Stratford.

▲
This is what New Place probably looked like during Shakespeare's ownership.

A Shakespeare Time Line

1564—William Shakespeare is baptized on April 26.

1582—He gets a license to marry Anne Hathaway in November.

1592—He is living in London. His first plays have been performed.

1592–1594—The bubonic plague spreads to London. Theaters close. Shakespeare turns to writing poetry.

1599—Shakespeare and six others buy the Globe theater. *Julius Caesar* is first performed.

1603—Queen Elizabeth I dies. The king of Scotland becomes James I of England.

1610—Shakespeare writes his last play, *The Tempest.*

1616—William Shakespeare dies on April 23.

Roman soldiers ▶

act one

ACT ONE, SCENE ONE

On a street in Rome on February 15, 44 B.C., a large crowd is celebrating Julius Caesar's victory over his enemy, Pompey. Flavius and Marullus, two government officials who supported Pompey, are angry. Marullus reminds the crowd that they used to like Pompey. The crowd leaves, and the two men take down the decorations honoring Caesar.

[*Enter* Flavius, Marullus, *and a large holiday crowd.*]

Flavius. [Flavius *is angry. He shouts at the crowd.*] Go home, you lazy people. Go to your homes! Is this a holiday? You all know that by law you are supposed to have your tools with you on a working day. [Flavius *speaks to one man in the crowd.*] Speak, what is your job?

Carpenter. Why, sir, I'm a carpenter.

Marullus. Where is your leather apron and your ruler? Why do you have your best clothes on?

[Marullus *turns to another man in the crowd.*] You, sir, what is your job?

Cobbler. To tell the truth, sir, I am just a cobbler.[1]

Marullus. But what is your job? Answer me quickly and clearly.

Cobbler. A job, sir, that I hope I may feel good about doing. I mend bad soles.[2]

Flavius. What is your job, you **knave**?[3] You worthless knave, what is your job?

Cobbler. No, I beg you, sir, don't be out with me; yet if you are out, sir, I can mend you.[4]

Marullus. What do you mean by that "Mend me," you disrespectful fellow?

Cobbler. Why, sir, cobble you.

Flavius. You are a cobbler?

Cobbler. True, sir. All I earn my living with is the awl.[5] I don't get into people's business, but I get

---

[1] cobbler—shoemaker, or someone who makes and mends shoes. *Wordplay*: Cobbler could also mean bungler, someone who messes things up.

[2] bad soles—*Wordplay*: The cobbler fixes the soles of shoes, but it might sound as though he fixes people's souls, their spirits.

[3] **knave**—servant or someone of low status.

[4] "Don't be out [of temper] with me; yet, if you are out [of shoes], sir, I can mend [your problem]."

[5] awl—*Wordplay*: "all" and "awl" sound the same. This is a pun, a joke playing on words that sound alike. An awl is a tool used by a cobbler to punch holes in leather.

into all. I am, sir, a doctor to old shoes. When they are in great danger, I patch them up. As good men as ever walked on leather have walked on my work.

Flavius. But why aren't you in your shop today? Why are you leading these men around the streets?

Cobbler. Truly, sir, to wear out their shoes, so I can have more work. But, really, sir, we have taken some time off to see Caesar, and to rejoice in his victory parade.

Marullus. [*He is angry again.*] Why are you celebrating? What **conquests**[6] does Caesar bring home? What conquered kings or rulers does he bring? You blocks, you stones, you worse than senseless things![7] O you hard hearts, you cruel men of Rome, didn't you know Pompey?[8] Often you climbed on walls, even to the tops of chimneys, with your babies in your arms. And you sat there all day so you could see great Pompey pass by you in the streets of Rome. And, when

---

[6] **conquests**—prizes won in war.

[7] blocks, stones worse than senseless things—Marullus says the crowd has no more feeling than a block of wood or a stone. They are worse than things that cannot sense (feel).

[8] Pompey—an outstanding Roman general and statesman. At first he was on Julius Caesar's side and then he turned against him. Caesar defeated Pompey in battle.

you saw his **chariot**[9] coming, didn't you all shout so loudly that the Tiber[10] shook with fear? And do you now put on your best clothes? And do you now have a holiday? And do you now throw flowers in front of Caesar who comes in victory over the blood of Pompey's sons? Be gone! Run to your houses, fall on your knees, pray to the gods to stop the punishment that must fall on you now!

Flavius. Go, go, good countrymen. Show you are sorry for the way you have acted, find others like yourselves and cry tears into the Tiber until you fill it to its highest level.

[*The crowd leaves.*]

Flavius. [*Speaking to* Marullus] See how even these low people can be made to feel as they should. They feel so guilty that they leave without saying a word. I want you to go down this road towards the Capitol.[11] I will go this other way. Take down any decorations that have been put up.

---

[9] **chariot**—a two-wheeled, horse-drawn cart, used for war or racing.

[10] Tiber—the river that flows through Rome.

[11] Capitol—temple on Capitoline hill, one of the seven hills on which ancient Rome was built.

Marullus. Is it all right for us to do that? It is the Feast of Lupercal.[12]

Flavius. I don't care. Tear down anything that looks like it celebrates Caesar's victory. I'll go through the city and drive the common people off the streets. If you see them gathered, send them away. We will pull out some of Caesar's feathers before he flies so high that he can swoop down on us at any time.

[*They exit.*]

---

[12] the Feast of Lupercal—a festival celebrated on February 15 to honor the god of fertility.

ACT ONE, SCENE TWO

In Rome, Caesar brings his wife Calpurnia to the race on the feast of Lupercal. In the crowd is a person who warns Caesar to beware the Ides of March (March 15). Cassius tries to turn Brutus against Caesar. Casca tells them that Antony has offered Caesar a crown three times, but Caesar refused it each time. He also reports that Flavius and Marullus lost their jobs for taking down the decorations. Brutus and Cassius agree to meet the next day. Cassius plans to leave fake letters for Brutus suggesting that the Romans want him to stop Caesar.

[*The trumpets sound. Enter* Caesar, Antony, Calpurnia, Portia, Decius Brutus, Cicero, Brutus, Cassius, *and* Casca. *They are followed by a crowd which includes a* Soothsayer, *a man who tells the future.*]

Caesar. Calpurnia!

Casca. Peace, I say! Caesar speaks.

Caesar. Calpurnia!

Calpurnia. Here, my lord.

Caesar. [*To* Calpurnia] Stand right in front of Antony when he runs the race. [Caesar *calls* Mark Antony.] Antony!

Antony. Caesar, my lord!

Caesar. Do not run so fast that you pass Calpurnia without touching her, Antony. You know the belief that a woman touched by a runner in this race will be more likely to have a child.

Antony. I shall remember. When Caesar says, "Do this!" it is done.

Caesar. Start, and do all the gods wish to be done.

Soothsayer. [*Shouting because of the noise of the crowd*] Caesar!

Caesar. What? Who calls me?

Casca. Everyone be silent! Be quiet!

Caesar. Who in the crowd calls my name? I hear a shrill voice through all the noise cry, "Caesar!" Speak, Caesar is turned to hear.

Soothsayer. Beware the Ides of March![1]

Caesar. What man is that?

---

[1] the Ides of March—March 15.

Brutus. A soothsayer who sees the future. He tells you to beware the Ides of March.

Caesar. Bring him to me. Let me see his face.

Cassius. [*Talking to the* Soothsayer.] Fellow, come here; look upon Caesar.

Caesar. What are you saying to me? Speak again.

Soothsayer. Beware the Ides of March!

Caesar. He is a dreamer. Let us leave him. Let us go.

[*A trumpet sounds. Everyone leaves except* Brutus *and* Cassius.]

Cassius. Will you watch the race?

Brutus. Not I.

Cassius. I beg you, watch.

Brutus. I am not interested in sports. I am not as full of energy as Antony is. Don't let me stop you, Cassius. I'll leave you.

Cassius. Brutus, I notice that you are not as friendly and as open with me as you have been in the past. You seem unfriendly to your friend.

Brutus. Cassius, don't be fooled. If I seem unfriendly, it is because I am upset, but not with you. I have recently been troubled with feelings and ideas that make me look unfriendly. But I don't wish my good friends to be unhappy, and you are a good friend. Don't think anything is wrong except that poor Brutus is at war with himself and forgets to be friendly to others.

Cassius. Then, Brutus, I really didn't understand how you were feeling. Because of that, I have not told you some important things. Tell me, good Brutus, can you see your face?

Brutus. No, Cassius, because the eye cannot see itself except in a reflection from something else.

Cassius. That's true. But it's sad, Brutus, that you don't have a good mirror that will show you how valuable you really are. I have heard many of the noblest men in Rome, except **immortal**[2] Caesar, speak of Brutus. They groan under the present problems and wish that noble Brutus could see himself as clearly as others see him.

Brutus. Into what dangers would you lead me, Cassius? You want me to see something in myself that is not there.

---

[2] **immortal**—everlasting. Caesar had been declared a god. Caesar, like a god, will live forever. Cassius is being ironic. He doesn't really think Caesar is godlike.

Cassius. I will tell you then, good Brutus. Since you know you cannot see yourself except by reflection, I will be your mirror. I will show you part of yourself that you don't know. Trust me, gentle Brutus. If I were a joker or made impossible promises to everyone I met, if I acted like a friend and then said bad things about my friends, or if I drank too much and then talked too much, then you would know that I was dangerous.

[*Trumpets sound and shouting is heard.*]

Brutus. What is this shouting about? I am afraid that the people are asking Caesar to be their king.

Cassius. Are you afraid? Then I think you don't wish Caesar to be king.

Brutus. I do not, Cassius, yet I think highly of him. But why are you keeping me here so long? What do you wish to say to me? If it is for the good of Rome, I wish to do what honor asks even if it means death. I love honor more than I fear death.

Cassius. I know you are honorable as well as I know what you look like, Brutus. Well, honor is what I'm talking about. I don't know what you and other men think about this life, but for me, I'd rather not be alive than live in fear of someone no greater than myself. I was born as free as Caesar; so were you. We both have fed as well as Caesar, and we both can stand the winter cold as well as he can.

One time, on a very cold and windy day, the Tiber river was flooded. Caesar said to me, "Cassius, do you dare jump into this flood and swim to that point?" When he said this, dressed as I was, I jumped into the freezing and flooded river and called out for him to follow me. He did. The river roared, and we fought against it with all our strength. But before we reached the point, Caesar cried, "Help me, Cassius, or I will sink!" Then I carried the tired Caesar out of the river. This Caesar is now called a god, and Cassius is a wretched creature and must bow down if Caesar only nods at him.

He had a fever when he was in Spain. When he was sickest, I noticed how he shook. It's true. This god did shake. His cowardly lips lost their color. And his eye, which the world is afraid of, lost its healthy look. I heard him groan. And his tongue, which told the Romans to write his speeches in their books, cried, "Give me something to drink," as if he were a sick girl. It amazes me that such a feeble man should have such a high place in this world and get the prizes all for himself.

[*A shout from the crowd offstage. Trumpets sound.*]

Brutus. Another cheer from all the people. I believe they are cheering some new honor they have given Caesar.

Cassius. Why, man, he stands across the world like a Colossus,[3] and we little men walk under his huge legs and peep around to find ourselves dishonorable graves.

Men at some time are masters of their fates.
The fault, dear Brutus, is not in our stars,
But in ourselves, that we are underlings.[4]

"Brutus" and "Caesar": Is "Caesar" a better name? Why should we hear "Caesar" more often? Write both names. Yours is as good a name. Say them. They sound as good. Does one name sound more important? Call up spirits with them: "Brutus" is as magical as "Caesar." Now in the name of all the gods at once, what

---

[3] Colossus—giant statue in Rhodes; anyone who is very powerful.

[4] underlings—unimportant people. These three famous lines are in Shakespeare's original words. Cassius is saying that if people don't succeed, they should not blame the stars, or fate, but should blame themselves.

does Caesar eat that has made him grow so great? We should all be ashamed! Rome, you no longer have great men! When has there ever been only one great man in Rome? When was there a time when people talked as if there was only one man who lived in Rome? Rome is still called Rome, but now there is room for only one man in Rome. O, you and I have heard our fathers say there used to be a Brutus[5] who would have let the devil live in Rome before he would let Rome be ruled by a king.

Brutus. I know you are my good friend. I trust you. I can guess a little about what you want me to do. I will tell you later what I am thinking. For now, if you are my friend, do not try to persuade me any more. I will think about what you have said carefully. I will find a time to hear and talk about such important matters. Until then, my noble friend, think about this: Brutus would rather live in an unknown village than live in Rome the way it is likely to be.

Cassius. I am glad my weak words have shown me that Brutus cares.

Brutus. The race is done, and Caesar is returning.

---

[5] Brutus had an ancestor, also named Brutus, who forced the last Roman king, Tarquin, to leave.

Cassius. As they pass by, pull Casca over here. He will tell us in his sour way what has happened today.

[*Enter* Caesar, *with* Antony *beside him, other followers, and* Casca *in the rear.*]

Brutus. [*Aside*[6] *to* Cassius] I will. But look, Cassius, Caesar looks angry. All the rest look like children who are in trouble. Calpurnia's cheeks are pale. Cicero[7] looks like he has not had his way in some political debate.

Cassius. [*Aside to* Brutus] Casca will tell us what is wrong.

[Caesar *glances at* Cassius, *then turns to* Antony.]

Caesar. Antony!

Antony. Caesar?

Caesar. [*Aside to* Antony] Let me have men around me who are fat, well cared for, and who sleep well every night. Cassius, over there, has a **lean**[8] and hungry look. He thinks too much. Such men are dangerous.

---

[6] *Aside*—This is a stage direction. It is used when the speaker is either speaking to himself or so that only a few people can hear.

[7] Cicero was a great politician and speaker.

[8] **lean**—thin.

Antony. [*Aside to* Caesar] Don't be afraid of him, Caesar. He's not dangerous. He is a noble Roman, an honorable man.

Caesar. [*Aside to* Antony] I wish he were fatter! But I am not afraid of him. Yet if I could be afraid of anyone, I don't know a man I should avoid as much as that skinny Cassius. He reads a lot. He sees everything. He knows why people act the way they do. He doesn't love plays, as you do, Antony. He doesn't listen to music. He doesn't smile much, and when he does smile, it's as if he were laughing at himself for smiling. Such men are never happy when they see someone greater than themselves, and that is why they are very dangerous. I tell you what is to be feared, but I do not fear because I am always Caesar. Come stand on my right side, for this ear is deaf. Tell me truly what you think of Cassius.

[*Trumpets sound.* Caesar *and the crowd with him exit, but* Brutus *stops* Casca.]

Casca. What do you want?

Brutus. Casca, tell us what happened today that made Caesar look so serious.

Casca. Why? You were with him, weren't you?

Brutus. I wouldn't have asked you what happened if I had been with him.

Casca. Why, they offered Caesar a crown. When it was offered, he pushed it away with the back of his hand, and then all the people started cheering him.

Brutus. What was the second shout for?

Casca. Why, for that too.

Cassius. They shouted three times. What was the last shout for?

Casca. Why, for that too.

Brutus. Did they offer him a crown three times?

Casca. Yes, indeed, they did. And three times he pushed it away, every time more gently than the last. And every time he pushed it away, my honest neighbors[9] cheered.

Cassius. Who offered Caesar the crown?

Casca. Why, Antony.

---

[9] my honest neighbors—Casca means the people around him in the crowd. Casca really doesn't like the common people, as you will see.

Brutus. Tell us about it, gentle Casca.

Casca. I can't explain what happened. I saw Mark Antony offer him a crown, but it wasn't really a crown. It was one of those **coronets.**[10] He pushed it away, but I think he wanted it. Then Antony offered it again. Caesar pushed it away again. But I think he hated to take his hands off it. And then Antony offered it a third time, and still he refused it a third time. The low-class crowd shouted and clapped their chapped hands and threw their sweaty caps in the air. Their breath was so bad when they shouted that it almost choked Caesar. He fainted and fell down. For my own part, I dared not laugh, for fear of opening my lips and breathing their bad breath.

Cassius. But wait a minute, I beg you! What? Did Caesar faint?

Casca. He fell down in the marketplace, and foamed at the mouth, and couldn't speak.

Brutus. He probably has the falling sickness.[11]

---

[10] **coronets**—small crowns or headbands. In Rome, a wreath of victory might be called a coronet.

[11] the falling sickness—epilepsy, a disease that can cause the sufferer to fall down and break into violent movement.

Cassius. No, Caesar doesn't have it. You and I and honest Casca, we have the falling sickness.[12]

Casca. I don't know what you mean by that, but I am sure Caesar fell down. The dirty, ragged people clapped and hissed him as he pleased and displeased them. They treated him like an actor in the theatre.

Brutus. When he got control of himself again, what did he say?

Casca. Before he fell down, when he saw the herd of people was glad, he pushed away the crown. Then he opened his coat and offered to let the people cut his throat if they wanted to. If I had been a working man, I would have done it. And then he fell. When he came to, he said if he had done or said anything wrong, he wanted their worships to think it was his sickness. Three or four low-class women near me cried, "Alas, poor soul," and forgave him with all their hearts. But I didn't pay any attention to them. If Caesar had stabbed their mothers, they would have said the same thing.

Brutus. And then he came away upset?

---

[12] the falling sickness—*Wordplay*: Cassius is using "the falling sickness" to mean that he, Casca, and Brutus are falling out of power because Caesar is taking all the power.

Casca. Yes.

Cassius. Did Cicero say anything?

Casca. Yes, he spoke Greek.

Cassius. What did he say?

Casca. How should I know? But those that understood him smiled at one another and shook their heads, but for me, it was Greek to me.[13] [Casca *starts to leave and then turns.*] I can tell you more news: Marullus and Flavius have lost their jobs for pulling decorations off Caesar's statues. Goodbye. There was more foolishness, if I could remember it.

Cassius. Will you have dinner with me tonight, Casca?

Casca. No, I have promised to go somewhere else.

Cassius. Will you eat with me tomorrow?

Casca. Yes, if I'm still alive, and you still ask me to, and your dinner is worth eating.

Cassius. Good, I will expect you.

---

[13] Cicero spoke Greek because he was educated in Greece, and Greek was the educated language of the time. Casca didn't understand Greek. "It was Greek to me" is still used to mean the speaker didn't understand what was being said.

Casca. Do so. Farewell to you both.

[Casca *exits.*]

Brutus. He doesn't seem as pleasant or as clever as I remember him in school.

Cassius. He is clever enough in doing what is brave and noble. He acts as if he were not as clever as he is. His slowness makes men listen better to his good words.

Brutus. So that's it. I will leave you for now. Tomorrow, if you wish to speak to me, I will come to your house, or if you wish, you may come to mine.

Cassius. I will do so. Until tomorrow, think about what is happening in Rome.

[*Exit* Brutus.]

Cassius. Well, Brutus, you are noble; yet I see I can use you. That's why noble people should stay with noble people. For who is so strong they can't be tricked? Caesar doesn't like me, but he loves Brutus. If I were Brutus now, and he were Cassius, I wouldn't listen to him. I will have several people write messages to Brutus. And tonight, I will have them thrown in his windows so they don't seem to have come from me. All the messages will say that people think he is honorable. They will hint at Caesar's love of power. After this, let Caesar think he is all-powerful, but we will shake him, or we will live through worse days.

[Cassius *exits.*]

ACT ONE, SCENE THREE

On March 14, there is a violent thunderstorm. Casca fears that the storm and other things predict terrible events to come. Cassius says Caesar is the cause and persuades Casca to join with others to stop Caesar. Cassius tells Cinna to put the fake letters where Brutus will find them. Cassius and Casca plan to visit Brutus later that night and talk him into joining them. If Brutus is on their side, people will think they are honorable.

[*Thunder and lightning.* Casca *enters with his sword drawn.* Cicero *enters from the other side.*]

Cicero. Good evening, Casca. Did you go with everyone back to Caesar's house? Why are you out of breath? Why do you stare like that?

Casca. Are you not upset when the earth shakes? O Cicero, I have seen storms when the howling winds have broken mighty oak trees, and I have seen the ocean rage and foam, trying to reach the sky. But never until tonight, never until now, did I see a storm raining fire. There must be war in heaven, or else the gods think the world is too evil and are trying to destroy it.

Cicero. Did you see something strange besides the storm?

Casca. A common slave—you'd know him if you saw him—held up his left hand, and his hand burned as if it were twenty candles, and yet his hand was unhurt. Besides—I have kept my sword out since I saw it—near the Capitol I met a lion who stared at me and went by me without hurting me. There were a hundred women huddled together who were so afraid they looked like ghosts. They swore they saw burning men walking up and down the streets. And during the day, the owl, the bird of night, came to the marketplace at noon hooting and shrieking. When all of these fearful and strange things happen together, something unnatural and terrible is about to happen. These are signs.

Cicero. Yes, it is a strange time. But different men will say these signs mean different things. Does Caesar go to the Capitol tomorrow?

Casca. He does. He told Antony to tell you he would be there tomorrow.

Cicero. Good night then, Casca. It's not good to walk in this storm.

Casca. Farewell, Cicero.

[Cicero *exits.* Cassius *enters.*]

Cassius. Who's there?

Casca. A Roman.

Cassius. Casca. I can tell by your voice.

Casca. You hear well. Cassius, what kind of night is this?

Cassius. A very good night for honest men.

Casca. Who ever saw such threatening skies?

Cassius. Those who have known the earth so full of faults. For my part, I have walked around the streets, giving myself to this dangerous night. I have not hidden myself from the storm. I have stood where the lightning could strike me. I tried to stand just where it would hit.

Casca. Why did you tempt the heavens so much? Men should be afraid when the gods send such dreadful messengers to us.

Cassius. You are foolish, Casca. You lack the courage a Roman should have, or you don't use it. You look pale and are afraid. You let yourself be surprised to see the strange anger of the heavens. But think about the true cause of this storm. Why all these fires and ghosts? Why do birds and beasts act so strangely; why do the **senile,**[1] fools, and children suddenly tell the future; why do all these things change from what they are normally to monstrous things? You will see that heaven has filled them with these powers to warn us that something terrible is about to happen. Now, Casca, I could name a man who is like this dreadful night that thunders and lightnings, opens graves, and roars like the lion does in the Capitol. He is a man no greater than you or me. But he has changed into something larger than a man, and should be as frightening as this storm and strange happenings.

Casca. You mean Caesar, don't you, Cassius?

Cassius. Let it be who it is, for Romans now are as strong as their ancestors, but these are sad times. Our fathers' minds are dead, and we have our mothers' spirits. We endure meekly because we are as weak as women.

---

[1] **senile**—old people suffering memory loss.

Casca. Indeed, they say that tomorrow the Senators will make Caesar king. He will be king on sea and land, in every place, except here in Italy.

Cassius. I know where I will put this dagger then. Cassius will free Cassius.[2] That is how the gods make the weak strong. That is how the gods defeat **tyrants.**[3] Neither a stony tower, metal walls, an airless prison, nor iron chains can hold the spirit. A life that is weary of this worldly prison can always let itself out. If I know this, let all the world also know I can get rid of any tyranny that I suffer.

Casca. So can I. Every prisoner has in his own hand the power to end his captivity.

Cassius. Why does Caesar wish to be a tyrant then? Poor man, I know he would not be a wolf, except he sees that Romans are sheep. He would not be a lion if we were not deer. If you wish to start a great fire, you begin with weak straws. What trash is Rome, what rubbish, what waste, when it is used to light the great fire of so bad a thing as Caesar. But oh Grief,[4] where

---

[2] Cassius means he will kill himself.

[3] **tyrants**—absolute rulers who govern in a cruel and unjust way.

[4] oh Grief—oh sadness. Cassius is talking about his feeling as if it were a person.

do you take me? Perhaps I am speaking to a willing prisoner. Then I will have to pay for my words. But I have a weapon, and I am not afraid of danger.

Casca. You speak to Casca. I do not betray my friends. Here's my hand. I promise that if you join a plan to stop all these evils, I will do as much as the person who does the most.

Cassius. [*They shake hands.*] We have made a deal. Then I want you to know, Casca, that already some of the noblest Romans have joined me in an action that is honorable and dangerous. They are waiting for me at the entrance to Pompey's theater. On this night of fearful storms, we cannot meet in the streets. The sky is red, like the work we must do. It is most bloody, fiery, and most terrible.

[*Enter* Cinna.]

Casca. Be careful. Someone is coming.

Cassius. It is Cinna. I recognize his walk. He is a friend. [*Calling out to* Cinna] Cinna, where are you going in such a hurry?

Cinna. To find you. Who's with you? Metellus Cimber?

Cassius. No, it is Casca. He has joined us. Is everyone waiting for me?

Cinna. Casca, I am glad you are with us. What a fearful night this is. Two or three of us have seen strange sights.

Cassius. Are they waiting for me? Tell me.

Cinna. Yes, they are. O Cassius, if you could only get the noble Brutus to join us—

Cassius. Relax. Good Cinna, take this paper and put it on the chair that Brutus uses when he judges. Throw this paper through his open window. Set this note on the statue of old Brutus.[5] When all this is done, meet me at Pompey's theater. Are Decius Brutus and Trebonius there?

Cinna. Everyone is there except Metellus Cimber. He went to your house to find you. Well, I will go put these papers where you have told me.

Cassius. When you have finished, go to Pompey's theater.

[Cinna *exits.*]

---

[5] Cassius is giving Cinna fake notes that seem to be from different people, but are all from Cassius. The notes will encourage Brutus to join the plans against Caesar.

Cassius. Come, Casca, before day comes we must see Brutus at his house. He is already three-quarters on our side. We will get him to join us now.

Casca. Everyone respects him. Anything we do that seems evil will, like magic, seem good when he supports us.

Cassius. You're right. You have understood his importance and how much we need him. Let us go. It's after midnight, and before day we will wake him and be sure he is with us.

[They exit.]

act two

ACT TWO, SCENE ONE

Before dawn on the Ides of March, Brutus can't sleep. He is worrying that Caesar may become king. Brutus's ancestor helped begin the Republic. Must he now kill Caesar to save the Republic? His servant brings him one of Cassius's letters. Cassius and his followers arrive. They talk about their plans. Cassius thinks Mark Antony should be killed as well. Brutus disagrees. After everyone leaves, Brutus's wife Portia enters. She wants to know why he is worried. He says he will tell her later and leaves to go to the Capitol.

[*Enter* Brutus.]

Brutus. Lucius, where are you? I cannot tell how late it is—Lucius, I say! (*To himself*) I wish I could sleep as well as that boy. (*Calling again*) When will you wake, Lucius? Awake, I say! Lucius!

[*Enter* Lucius.]

Lucius. Did you call me, my lord?

Brutus. Take a candle to my study, Lucius. When it is ready, call me.

Lucius. I will, my lord.

[Lucius *exits.*]

Brutus. [Brutus *is speaking to himself.*[1]] He[2] must die. For myself, I have no personal reason to want his death. It would be for the good of Rome. He wants to be king. How would being king make him different? There's the question. Poisonous snakes come out in the sunshine, and then everyone must be careful where they walk. If we crown him, we will have given him the power to sting us. Greatness is spoiled when it separates a man's sense of guilt from his use of power. To tell the truth, Caesar's thinking is not ruled by his emotions. It's common for a man to act humbly when he climbs the ladder to power, and then, when he reaches the top, to turn away from **humility**.[3] So may Caesar. We must prevent that. We must think he

[1] The speech that comes next is a *soliloquy*, a long, uninterrupted speech in which the character is thinking out loud.

[2] He—Caesar.

[3] **humility**—not being proud and feeling above everyone else.

is like the poisonous snake's egg, which if it hatches, will do harm. We must kill him in the shell.

[*Enter* Lucius.]

Lucius. The candle is burning in your study, sir. I found this note under your window. I'm sure it wasn't there when I went to bed. [Lucius *gives* Brutus *the note.*]

Brutus. Go to bed again. It isn't day yet. Isn't tomorrow the Ides of March?

Lucius. I don't know, sir.

Brutus. Look at the calendar and tell me.

Lucius. I will, sir.

[Lucius *exits.*]

Brutus. Meteors make the sky so bright that I can read this. [*He opens the note and reads.*] "Brutus, you sleep: awake, and see yourself. Shall Rome, and so on:[4] Speak, strike, make things right." I have had many of these notes recently. They all ask if Rome should be ruled by one man. What, Rome? My ancestors drove the last Roman king

---

[4] and so on—Brutus is reading a note that says things he has read in other, similar letters. It is one of Cassius's faked letters aimed at getting Brutus to join in the murder of Caesar.

out of the city. Am I begged to speak and strike? O Rome, I promise you, if things will be right, I will do all you ask.

[*Enter* Lucius.]

Lucius. Sir, tomorrow is the Ides of March.

[*Offstage knocking.*]

Brutus. Thank you. Go to the gate. Someone is knocking.

[Lucius *exits.*]

Brutus. Since Cassius first started me thinking about Caesar, I have not slept. The time between thinking about a dreadful thing and doing it is like a horrible dream or nightmare. The spirit and the body fight each other, like a small kingdom in a civil war.

[*Enter* Lucius.]

Lucius. Sir, it is your brother Cassius[5] at the door. He wishes to see you.

Brutus. Is he alone?

Lucius. No, sir, there are more men with him.

Brutus. Do you know them?

---

[5] brother Cassius—Cassius was married to Brutus's sister.

Lucius. No, sir. Their hats are pulled down and their collars pulled up, so it is hard to see their faces.

Brutus. Let them enter.

[*Exit* Lucius.]

Brutus. These are the men who are working against Caesar. Are you ashamed to be seen even at night when evil things come out? Then, when it is day, how will you find a cave dark enough to hide your ugliness? Do not hide in darkness. Hide in smiles. Look friendly. For if you look like what you are about to do, even hell could not hide you from those who wish to stop you.

[*Enter the conspirators:* Cassius, Casca, Decius Brutus, Cinna, Metellus Cimber, *and* Trebonius.]

Cassius. I am sorry we have disturbed your sleep. Good morning, Brutus. Do we trouble you?

Brutus. I have been awake all night. Do I know these men who are with you?

Cassius. Yes, every one of them. And every man here honors you. Every one wishes that you valued yourself as much as every noble Roman values you. This is Trebonius.

Brutus. He is welcome here.

Cassius. This, Decius Brutus.

Brutus. He is welcome too.

Cassius. This Casca; this, Cinna; and this, Metellus Cimber.

Brutus. They are all welcome. What troubles keep you all awake so late?

Cassius. Could I speak to you in private?[6]

[Cassius *and* Brutus *step away from the group and whisper.]*

Decius. This is east. Doesn't the sun come up in this direction?

Casca. No.

Cinna. Pardon me, but it does. And the gray lines in the sky are the start of daybreak.

Casca. You are both wrong. Here where I point my sword is where the sun will come up. It is in a southerly direction because of spring. Two months from now it will come up further north. Due east is over there where the Capitol is.

---

[6] Cassius sees that Brutus is being very careful. He does not know how far to trust these men, or what he is to do. Cassius explains things to Brutus.

[Brutus *rejoins the group quickly.*]

Brutus. Give me your hands, all of you, one by one.

[Brutus *quickly goes around and shakes each man's hand.*]

Cassius. And let us swear that we will do what we say.

Brutus. No, not an oath. The trustworthy look of these men today, the patient suffering of our souls, the evil times—if these are not reason enough to do what we will do, then stop now. Let every man go home to his empty bed. Let tyranny go on, and let every man die when the tyrant decides. If these reasons are strong enough to make cowards and women act, then, my countrymen, we don't need anything but our cause to make us act. What other tie joins us than we are Romans who can keep a secret? We have agreed on a plan and will not go back on our agreement. And what other oath do we need than our promises to each other? What we have planned will happen, or we will die for it. Let priests and cowards and deceitful men and those who cannot be trusted swear. But do not stain the perfect goodness of our cause or the strength of our spirits by asking us to swear an oath to do what we are going to do. Every drop of blood that every Roman has, and nobly has, shows that he is guilty of an act not truly Roman if he breaks the smallest part of a promise that he makes.

Cassius. What about Cicero? Shall we see if he will join us? I think he would stand strongly with us.

Casca. Let's not leave him out.

Cinna. No, by no means.

Metellus. O, let us ask him. His age and silver hair will buy us good opinions. People will say that he planned this. Our youth and wildness will be covered by his seriousness.

Brutus. O, don't ask him.[7] Let's not tell him our plans. He will never do anything that other men plan.

Cassius. Then leave him out.

Casca. Indeed, he is not fit.

Decius. Shall no one else be touched?[8]

---

[7] Brutus and Cicero did not get along.

[8] touched—killed.

Cassius. Decius, that's a good idea. I don't think it's right that Mark Antony, so well loved by Caesar, should live longer than Caesar. We shall find him very good at working against us. If he uses all his power against us, he may be able to hurt us. Let Antony and Caesar fall together.

Brutus. Our plan will seem too bloody, Cassius, to cut the head off and then hack the **limbs**[9] off too. We would look angry and jealous. Antony is only a limb of Caesar. Let us be priests sacrificing, not butchers, Cassius. We will fight the spirit of Caesar, and in the spirit of men there is no blood. I wish we could beat his spirit without cutting him up! But, I am sorry, Caesar must bleed! And, gentle friends, let's kill him boldly, but not in anger. Let's cut him like meat we are serving to the gods, not like meat for the dogs. Let our hearts command our hands to do this, and afterwards be sorry that we had to do it. People will see that we were forced to do this. The ordinary people will see that we are cleaning, not murdering. And, as for Mark Antony, don't think about him. He can do no more harm than Caesar's arm after Caesar's head is cut off.

---

[9] **limbs**—arms and legs.

Cassius. Yet I fear him, because he deeply loves Caesar—[Brutus *interrupts* Cassius.]

Brutus. Alas, good Cassius, do not think about him. If he loves Caesar so much, he could die for Caesar, but he won't. He's not serious enough. He loves sports, wildness, and crowds of friends.

Trebonius. There's no reason to fear him. Don't kill him. He will live and laugh with us in the future.

[*The clock strikes.*[10]]

Brutus. Peace, what time is it?

Cassius. It's three in the morning.

Trebonius. It's time to go.

Cassius. But Caesar may not go to the Capitol today. He has changed recently and has grown very superstitious. It may be that all the strange things that have been seen in this storm tonight and the advice he receives may keep him at home.

---

[10] There were no clocks to strike in ancient Rome. Shakespeare doesn't care. For him, everything really takes place in his own time.

Decius. Don't worry. If he decides to stay at home, I can make him change his mind. He loves to hear how everyone else can be tricked. I tell him he hates flattery, and then he is most flattered, and I trick him. Let me work on him. I know him. I will get him to go to the Capitol.

Cassius. We will all be there to fetch him.

Brutus. By eight o'clock. No later.

Cinna. No later than eight. Be there on time.

Metellus. Caius Ligarius hates Caesar because Caesar scolded him in public when Caius spoke well of Pompey. I'm surprised no one has thought of asking him to join us.

Brutus. Now, good Metellus, go to his house. He is a good friend of mine. I have already talked to him a little about this. Send him here, and I will get him to join us.

Cassius. It is morning. We'll leave you, Brutus. And, friends, go home, but remember what you have said, and show yourselves true Romans.

Brutus. Good gentlemen, look fresh and cheerful. Don't let our looks give away what we are going to do. Be like our Roman actors: act like nothing is wrong or unusual. And so, good morning to you all.

[*Exit all but* Brutus.]

Brutus. Boy! Lucius! Fast asleep? It doesn't matter. Enjoy your sweet young sleep! You don't have the plans and fantasies that the busy day puts in the brains of men; that's why you sleep so soundly.

[*Enter* Portia, *Brutus's wife.*]

Portia. Brutus, my lord!

Brutus. Portia! What's the matter? Why are you up so early? It's not good for you in your bad health to be getting up on these cold damp mornings.

Portia. It's not good for your health either. You have unlovingly left my bed, Brutus, and last night at supper you suddenly got up and walked around thinking, sighing, and looking very worried. When I asked you what was wrong, you gave me an angry look. I asked you again, and you scratched your head and impatiently stamped your foot. I insisted that you tell me what was wrong, but you would not answer. You angrily waved your hand and told me to leave. So I did, fearing to make you angrier. I was hoping you were just in a bad mood. Everyone has bad moods. They will not let you eat, or talk, or sleep. But if this bad mood changes your looks as much as it has changed the way you act, I will not know you. Brutus, my dear lord, tell me what is causing your grief.

Brutus. I'm not feeling very well. That's all.

Portia. You are wise. If you were not well, you would do what needs to be done to get your health back.

Brutus. I am doing that. Good Portia, go to bed.

Portia. If you are sick, is it good for you to walk without a coat on a cold, wet morning? If you are sick, will you leave your warm bed to walk in the cold, unhealthy night, to let the night air add to your sickness? No, my Brutus, you have some unnatural trouble in your mind. I am your wife. I should know what is bothering you. On my knees [Portia *kneels in front of* Brutus.] I beg you, if you ever thought me beautiful, by all your love promises, and by our marriage vow that made us one person, tell me, your other half, why you are so sad and worried. Who were the men who were here tonight? I saw six or seven men who hid their faces even in the darkness.

Brutus. Do not kneel, gentle Portia.

Portia. I would not need to kneel if you were gentle,[11] Brutus. Is there some secret that you can keep in our marriage? Tell me, Brutus. Have we been made one person in marriage? Or is there some limit to our marriage? Am I just to keep you company, comfort you, and share your bed? Do I just live on the edge of your love and trust? If that is so, I am merely Brutus's lover, not his wife.

Brutus. You are my true and honorable wife. You are as dear to me as the red drops of blood that go through my sad heart.

Portia. If this is true, then you should tell me this secret. I know I am a woman, but I am a woman that lord Brutus married. I admit I am a woman. But I have a good reputation: I am Cato's daughter.[12] I am stronger than most women

---

[11] gentle—*Wordplay*: Brutus uses the word *gentle* to mean soft, kind, sweet. Portia uses the same word to mean "be a gentleman," do everything a good man should do, tell his wife the truth.

[12] Cato was a great philosopher, general, and politician who was famous for his truthfulness. He supported Pompey against Julius Caesar. When Caesar won, Cato killed himself.

because of my father and my husband. Tell me your plans. I will not tell them to anyone else. I have proved that I can keep silent. I stabbed myself here on my leg. If I can stand that without saying anything, then I can keep my husband's secrets.

Brutus. O you gods, make me worthy of this noble wife!

[*There is knocking offstage.*]

Brutus. Listen! Someone knocks! Portia, go inside for a while. Soon your heart shall share the secrets of my heart. I will tell you all my plans. I will tell you what caused all my frowns. But, leave me quickly now.

[Portia *exits.*]

Brutus. Lucius, who is knocking?

[Lucius *enters with* Ligarius.]

Lucius. This sick man wishes to speak to you.

Brutus. Is it Caius Ligarius, that Metellus talked about? Boy, stand back. Caius Ligarius, are you all right?

Ligarius. I am sick, but I wish you a good morning.

Brutus. O what a time you have chosen, noble Caius, to be sick. I wish you were not sick!

Ligarius. I am not sick if Brutus is doing something honorable and needs my help.

Brutus. I am doing something honorable and would need your help, Ligarius, if you were well.

Ligarius. By all the gods that Romans bow before, I throw away my sickness! Soul of Rome, brave son, born from noble ancestors, you, like a magician, have called back my dead spirit. Now tell me to run, and I will try to do impossible things. Yes, I will do impossible things. What's to do?

Brutus. A piece of work that will make sick men healthy.

Ligarius. [*Slyly*] But aren't some healthy that we must make sick?

Brutus. We must do that also. What we will do, my Caius, I will tell you as we are going to the person to whom it must be done.

Ligarius. Start, and with a heart newly full of energy, I will follow you. I don't know what we will do, but it is good enough that Brutus tells me to do it.

Brutus. Follow me then.

[*They exit.*]

ACT TWO, SCENE TWO

At his house, Caesar gets ready to go to the Capitol. Calpurnia thinks the strange signs she sees mean that Caesar will be harmed. She begs him to stay home. The priests, too, advise Caesar to stay home. He agrees. Then, after Decius Brutus arrives, Caesar decides he will not lie and say he is sick. Decius flatters Caesar and tells him that the Senate will crown him today. His enemies arrive, and so does Mark Antony. Caesar believes he is among friends.

[*Thunder and lightning. Enter* Caesar *in his sleeping clothes.*]

Caesar. Neither heaven nor earth has been at peace tonight. Three times in her sleep Calpurnia shouted, "Help us here! They murder Caesar!" [*A* Servant *enters.*] Who's that?

Servant. My lord?

Caesar. Go, tell the priests to make a sacrifice to the gods, and tell me what they think of my chances for success today.[1]

Servant. I will, my lord.

Calpurnia. What are you doing, Caesar? Are you thinking about leaving here today? You must not go out of this house today.

Caesar. I will go out. The only things that ever threatened me were looking at my back. When I face them, they run away.

Calpurnia. Caesar, I never paid much attention to signs,[2] yet now they frighten me. Besides the strange things that we have seen and heard, the watch[3] has seen horrible sights. A lioness gave birth in the middle of the street. Graves have opened, and the dead have walked. Fierce, fiery warriors fought in the clouds in military formation, as if there were a real war. And blood rained on the Capitol. Battle noises filled the air; horses neighed and men groaned. Ghosts shrieked and squealed in the streets. O

---

[1] The priests would sacrifice a small animal, then they would cut it open and look at its insides. They were supposed to be able to see into the future this way.

[2] Many societies have believed that when a great man, like Caesar, is going to die or does die, then nature in sympathy shows unusual signs.

[3] the watch—the night policeman.

Caesar, these things are beyond all ordinary happenings, and I am afraid.

Caesar. We cannot stop what the mighty gods have planned. Even with these strange things happening, I will go to the Capitol today. These predictions are for everyone, not just for Caesar.

Calpurnia. No comets are seen when beggars die. The heavens do strange things when kings die.

Caesar. Cowards die many times before their deaths; brave men taste death only once.[4] Of all the strange things I have heard, it seems to me the strangest that men should fear death, seeing that everyone must die. Death will come when it comes, and no one can do anything about it.

[*The* Servant *enters.*]

Caesar. What do the priests who can see into the future have to say?

Servant. They don't want you to leave the house today. When they pulled the **entrails**[5] out of the offering, they could not find the animal's heart.

Caesar. The gods do this to make cowards feel ashamed. Caesar would be a beast without a

---

[4] Cowards die many times in their imaginations. Brave men know death only when they actually die.

[5] **entrails**—heart, liver, intestines, etc.

heart if he stayed at home today because he was afraid. No, Caesar shall not stay at home. Danger knows full well that Caesar is more dangerous than danger. Danger and I are two lions born on the same day. I am the older and more terrible. Caesar shall go out.

Calpurnia. Alas, my lord, your wisdom is destroyed by your confidence. Do not leave the house today. Say it is my fear that keeps you in the house and not your own. We'll send Mark Antony to the Senate. He shall say you are sick. I beg you on my knees, let me have my way in this.

Caesar. [*Reluctantly*] Mark Antony shall say I am sick, and because of your fear I shall stay at home.

[*Enter* Decius Brutus.]

Caesar. Here's Decius Brutus; he shall take the message.

Decius. Caesar, all hail! Good morning, worthy Caesar. I come to take you to the Senate House.

Caesar. And you have come just at the right time. You can take my greetings to the Senators and tell them I will not come there today. Cannot come there is false. That I dare not come there is falser. I will not come today; tell them so, Decius.

Calpurnia. Say he is sick.

Caesar. Shall Caesar tell a lie? Have I fought in so many battles in so many faraway places and be afraid to tell old men the truth? Decius, go tell them, Caesar will not come.

Decius. Most mighty Caesar, tell me some reason or I will be laughed at when I tell them this.

Caesar. The reason is my decision. I will not come. That is enough to satisfy the Senate. But I will tell you because you are my friend. Calpurnia here, my wife, keeps me at home. She dreamed that she saw my statue like a fountain with a hundred spouts running with pure blood. Many happy Romans were smiling and bathing their hands in the blood. Calpurnia thinks this is a warning that something evil is about to happen. She has begged me on her knees to stay home today.

Decius. [*Thinking quickly*] She didn't understand the dream. It was a good and lucky dream. Your statue pouring blood from many pipes with many smiling Romans washing their hands means something else. It means that from you great Rome shall get new blood to make her strong and that great men shall crowd around to get favors from you. That is what Calpurnia's dream meant.

Caesar. That is a good explanation of the dream.

Decius. It is, when you have heard what I have to say. The Senate has decided to give a crown today to mighty Caesar. If you send them word that you will not come, they may change their minds. Besides, they might think you were making fun of them if someone said, "Break up the Senate until another time when Caesar's wife has better dreams." If Caesar hides himself, won't they whisper, "Look, Caesar is afraid"? Pardon me, Caesar, but because I love you so much and hope for your success, I have to tell you this. I know I shouldn't, but you are my friend.

Caesar. How foolish your fears seem now, Calpurnia! I am ashamed I gave in to them. Give me my toga.[6] I will go.

[*Enter* Brutus, Ligarius, Metellus Cimber, Casca, Trebonius, Cinna, *and* Publius.]

---

[6] toga—the outer garment worn by the ancient Roman men. It was a simple piece of cloth that covered the body except for the right arm.

Caesar. And look, Publius has come to take me to the Senate.

Publius. Good morning, Caesar.

Caesar. Welcome, Publius. What, Brutus, are you up so early too? Good morning, Casca. Caius Ligarius, the sickness that makes you so thin is more your enemy than Caesar is. What time is it?

Brutus. Caesar, it is eight o'clock.

Caesar. I thank you all for your pains and courtesy.

[*Enter* Antony.]

Caesar. See, Antony, who parties all night, is up. Good morning, Antony.

Antony. The same to most noble Caesar.

Caesar. Tell the servants to put out the wine. I am to blame for waiting so long. Now, Cinna, Metellus! What, Trebonius, I have to speak with you for at least an hour. Remember to speak to me later. Stay near me so I will remember to speak to you.

Trebonius. Caesar, I will. [*Aside to himself*] I will be so near you that your best friends will wish I had been further away.

Caesar. My good friends, go in, and taste some wine with me. And we, like friends, will soon leave together.

Brutus. [*Aside to himself*] "Like friends." I am sad to think that "like" doesn't mean to me what it means to you, O Caesar. Thinking about it makes me sad.

ACT TWO, SCENE THREE

On a street near the Capitol, Artemidorus reads his note warning Caesar about the plot. He plans to pass the note to Caesar as he goes by.

Artemidorus. [*Reading his own note.*]

"Caesar, beware of Brutus. Pay attention to Cassius. Do not go near Casca. Keep an eye on Cinna. Do not trust Trebonius. Carefully watch Metellus Cimber. Decius Brutus is not your friend. You have wronged Caius Ligarius. All of these men wish to do one thing, and it is to hurt Caesar. If you can be killed, watch out. A man who thinks himself secure will not be careful. The mighty gods defend you.

Your friend, Artemidorus."

I will wait until Caesar comes past here. Then I will give him this. I am sad that virtue cannot live without being torn apart by jealousy. If you read this, O Caesar, you may live. If not, fate helps traitors.

[Artemidorus *exits.*]

ACT TWO, SCENE FOUR

In front of Brutus's house, Portia sends Lucius to the Capitol to find out what's happening. She talks to a person who plans to warn Caesar. He is a soothsayer, someone who claims to see the future. Portia worries about Brutus's part in the plot.

[*Enter* Portia *and* Lucius.]

Portia. I pray you, boy, run to the Senate House. Don't stay to talk to me. Go. Why are you staying?

Lucius. To know what you want me to do.

Portia. You could get there and back here before I can think of what to tell you to do. [*Aside to herself*] I must be calm. There must be a huge mountain between what my heart knows and what I say. I have a man's mind, but a woman's physical strength. How hard it is for women to keep a secret![1] [*To* Lucius] Are you still here?

---

[1] Brutus has obviously told Portia about the plot.

Lucius. Madam, what should I do? Run to the Capitol, and nothing else? And then return to you, and nothing else?

Portia. Yes, bring me word, boy, if your lord Brutus looks well. He was sick when he left. And notice carefully what Caesar does. See who crowds up to him to ask favors. Listen, boy, what is that noise?

Lucius. I don't hear any noise, madam.

Portia. I pray you, listen carefully! I hear something that sounds like the confused noise of a battle. The sound seems to come from the Capitol.

Lucius. Truly, madam, I don't hear anything.

[*The* Soothsayer *enters.*]

Portia. Come here, fellow! Where did you come from?

Soothsayer. From my own house, good lady.

Portia. What time is it?

Soothsayer. About nine, lady.

Portia. Has Caesar gone to the Capitol yet?

Soothsayer. Madam, not yet. I am going now to see him pass by.

Portia. You have some favor to ask Caesar?

Soothsayer. That I have, lady, if it will please Caesar to be so good to Caesar as to hear me. I shall ask him to be a good friend to himself.

Portia. Why? Do you know that someone is planning to harm Caesar?

Soothsayer. I don't know that they will harm him, but I am afraid something might happen. Good morning to you! Here the street is narrow. The crowd that follows so close to Caesar—the Senators, judges, favor-seekers—will crowd a weak man like me almost to death. I'll get to a place with more room, and there I will speak to great Caesar when he comes.

[*The* Soothsayer *exits.*]

Portia. I must go inside. Oh, me! How weak is the heart of a woman! O Brutus, the heavens give you success in your business today. [*Aside to herself*] I am sure the boy heard me. [*To* Lucius] Brutus is going to ask Caesar for a favor that Caesar will not grant. [*Aside to herself*] O, I feel faint! Run, Lucius, and give my greetings to my lord Brutus. Say I am all right, then come back to me, and tell me what he says.

[Lucius *exits.*]

act three

ACT THREE, SCENE ONE

Outside the Capitol, the soothsayer and Artemidorus try to warn Caesar. Caesar goes into the Capitol. His enemies surround him, pretending to plead for Metellus Cimber's brother. Suddenly, they rush Caesar and stab him to death. Mark Antony flees. Brutus persuades the murderers not to hurt Mark Antony. He says that he will explain the killing to the Roman people and that Antony should speak at Caesar's funeral. When Antony is left alone with Caesar's dead body, he vows revenge.

[*Enter* Caesar, Cassius, Casca, Decius Brutus, Brutus, Metellus Cimber, Trebonius, Cinna, Antony, Lepidus, Artemidorus, Publius, Popilius, *and the* Soothsayer.]

Caesar. [*Aside to the* Soothsayer] The Ides of March are here.

Soothsayer. Yes, but they are not gone.

Artemidorus. Hail Caesar! Read this note!

Decius. [*Afraid that the note will give them away*] Trebonius begs you to read his humble **suit**[1] when you have time.

Artemidorus. O Caesar, read mine first. My suit concerns you personally. Read it, great Caesar.

Caesar. [*Loudly, so the crowd can hear*] What concerns us personally shall be taken care of last.

Artemidorus. Do it now, Caesar. Read it right now.

Caesar. What, is he mad?

Publius. Sirrah,[2] get out of the way.

Cassius. Why are you trying to give your **petition**[3] to Caesar on the street? Come to the Capitol like everyone else.

[Caesar *goes into the Senate House. The rest follow.*]

Popilius. [*Aside to some of Caesar's enemies*] I wish your business today may be successful.

Cassius. What business, Popilius?

Popilius. I hope you do well.

---

[1] **suit**—a legal paper asking for something.

[2] Sirrah—a way of addressing someone below the speaker's social level.

[3] **petition**—a written paper asking for a favor.

Brutus. What did Popilius Lena say?

Cassius. He wished us success in our business today. I am afraid that our plan has been found out.

Brutus. Look, he is going to speak to Caesar. Watch him.

Cassius. Casca, be ready to act quickly. We may have been found out. Brutus, what shall we do? I will not stop. I will either kill Caesar or myself.

Brutus. Cassius, calm down. Popilius Lena is not talking about us. Look, he is smiling, and Caesar is not upset.

Cassius. It is time for Trebonius to do his part. Look, he is getting Mark Antony out of the way.

[Antony *and* Trebonius *exit.*]

Decius. Where is Metellus Cimber? Tell him to ask Caesar for a favor right now.

Brutus. He is doing it. Get close to Caesar and join Cimber in his request.

Cinna. Casca, you are the first to strike Caesar.

[Caesar *talks to the crowd.*]

Caesar. Are we all ready? What is wrong that Caesar and his Senate can make right?

Metellus. Most high, most mighty, most powerful Caesar, Metellus Cimber bows before you with a humble heart—

Caesar. I must stop you, Cimber. This bowing and begging might flatter an ordinary man, and he might view the law as a children's game where the rules can be changed at any time. Don't be foolish and think Caesar will change the laws. I will not destroy justice by listening to the things that affect fools—flattery, bows, and sweet words. The law said your brother should be sent away. If you bow and beg and flatter for him, I will kick you out of my way like I would kick a dog in the street. I want you to understand this: Caesar does not do wrong, and without a very good reason Caesar will not change a sentence.

Metellus. Please, isn't there someone who can speak more sweetly to Caesar and ask that my brother be allowed to return?

Brutus. I kiss your hand, Caesar, but not to flatter you. I wish that Metellus Cimber's brother, Publius, might be freed from his sentence and allowed to return to Rome.

Caesar. What, Brutus!

Cassius. Pardon me, Caesar; Caesar, pardon me. I fall on the ground to beg you to allow Publius Cimber to return a free citizen.

Caesar. I would change my mind, if I were like you. If prayers could soften me, then your prayers would soften me. But I am as constant as the North Star.[4] It doesn't move or change. It has not equal in the sky. Of all the uncountable stars in the skies, there's only one star that never changes its place. It is the same in the world. There are many men in the world. Men are flesh and blood, and fearful; yet of all men, I know only one that holds his place without moving. I am that person. Let me prove it in this: I was certain that Cimber should be **banished**,[5] and I am certain he should remain banished.

Cinna. O Caesar—

Caesar. Go away! Will you lift up Olympus![6]

Decius. Great Caesar—

---

[4] The North Star, or polar star, always appears to be right over the North Pole.

[5] **banished**—forced to leave the country.

[6] Olympus—the mountain that was the home of the Greek and Roman gods. Of course, no one could move it because the gods wouldn't let them.

Caesar. I will not do this when Brutus asks. Why would I do it when anyone else asks?

Casca. My hands will do my speaking.

[Casca *stabs* Caesar, *then the other conspirators join in.* Brutus *is the last to stab* Caesar.]

Caesar. Et tu Brute?[7] Then fall Caesar.

[Caesar *dies. People run and scream in fear. Even Caesar's enemies are confused.*]

Cinna. Liberty! Freedom! Tyranny is dead! Run, shout it, tell everyone in the streets.

Cassius. Some of you go to the platforms where announcements are made to the common people. Cry out "Liberty, freedom, and **enfranchisement**!"[8]

Brutus. People, Senators, do not be afraid: don't run away. Stay here. Caesar was ambitious. He has paid for it with his life.

Casca. Speak to the people, Brutus.

Decius. And Cassius too.

---

[7] Et tu Brute?—"And you, Brutus?" in Latin. Caesar means, "And you, Brutus, are you also against me?" These were supposed to be the real Caesar's last words. Shakespeare kept them in Latin because they were so well known.

[8] **enfranchisement**—the right to vote. Since Caesar is dead, he cannot be king. The Republic will continue, and those who got to vote before will still vote.

Brutus. Where's Publius?[9]

Cinna. Here. He is confused and upset at this uproar.

Metellus. Stay together, or some friend of Caesar's may try to hurt—

Brutus. We don't need to defend ourselves. Publius, do not be afraid. No one plans to hurt you, or any other Roman. Tell the Senators, Publius.

Cassius. And leave us, Publius. If the people attack us, they might hurt you as well.

Brutus. Do so. Let no man stay here or suffer for this deed except we who did it.

[*Enter* Trebonius.]

Cassius. Where is Antony?

Trebonius. He has run to his house and is confused. Men, wives, and children stare, cry, and run as if it were the end of the world.

Brutus. Fate, we wait to see what you will do to us. We know we will die. We just don't know when, and we wish to die later.

---

[9] Publius is a senator, but also a very old man. He couldn't run away.

Casca. Why, he that cuts off twenty years of life, cuts off twenty years of fearing death.

Brutus. If that is true, then death is a **benefit.**[10] Then we are Caesar's friends. We have shortened the time he had to fear death. Kneel, Romans, kneel, and let us bathe our hands in Caesar's blood up to the elbows, and smear our swords. Then we will go to the marketplace, waving our bloody swords over our heads. Let's all cry, "Peace, freedom, liberty!"

Cassius. Kneel then, and wash your hands in his blood. How many hundreds of years from now shall this important scene be acted again,[11] in countries that have not been born yet and in languages we don't know?

Brutus. How many times shall Caesar bleed in a play who now is really bleeding at the foot of Pompey's statue, no more important than the dust?

Cassius. As often as that will be, that's how often we will be called the men that gave their country liberty.

---

[10] **benefit**—useful aid, advantage, help.

[11] This is a common thought of Shakespeare. Characters in his plays remind the audience about the theater. They even remind the audience that they are watching a play.

Decius. Shall we leave now?

Cassius. Yes, every man go. Brutus shall lead, and we will honor him by following with the boldest and best hearts in Rome.

[*A* Servant *enters.*]

Brutus. Wait, who is this? A friend of Antony.

Servant. Brutus, my master told me to kneel in front of you. Mark Antony told me to fall down, and, lying on the ground, to say: Brutus is noble, wise, brave, and honorable; Caesar was mighty, bold, generous, and loving. Say I love Brutus, and I honor him. Say, I feared Caesar, honored him, and loved him. If Brutus will promise that Antony may safely come to him and that Brutus will explain why Caesar had to die, Mark Antony shall not love dead Caesar as well as he loves the living Brutus. Antony will follow the fortunes and orders of noble Brutus in this new government. He will be loyal to you. So says Mark Antony.

Brutus. Your master is a wise and brave Roman. I never thought him less than that. Tell him, if he will come to this place, we will tell him why we did this. And I promise, he will leave safely.

Servant. I'll bring him here quickly.

[*The* Servant *exits.*]

Brutus. I know he will be our good friend.

Cassius. I hope you are right. But I am afraid of what he might do. There are real reasons to fear him, and my fears are always right.

[*Enter* Antony.]

Brutus. Here comes Antony. [*To* Antony] Welcome, Mark Antony.

Antony. [Antony *sees* Caesar's *dead body.*] O mighty Caesar! Have you fallen so low? Is this all that's left of your victories, glories, triumphs, and **spoils**?[12] Farewell. [Antony *turns to the murderers, who are bloody and have their swords out.*] I don't know, gentlemen, what you are planning to do, who else is too powerful. If you are going to kill me, there is no better time than the hour of Caesar's death. There is no weapon of half the worth of your swords, made rich with the most noble blood in all this world. I beg you, if you hate me, now while your hands are red with his hot blood, do what you wish. If I live a thousand years, I shall not find myself

---

[12] **spoils**—things won in wars.

so ready to die. No place will be better, no way of death better, as here by Caesar's body, and by you cut off,[13] the best and most powerful men of our time.

Brutus. O Antony! Don't beg us to kill you! I know we must look bloody and cruel because of our bloody hands and what we have done. You can see that. Yet all you see is our hands and this bloody business. You cannot see our hearts. They are filled with pity. We also pity Rome. We did what was best for Rome, even though it was something we did not wish to do. For your part, our swords cannot hurt you, Mark Antony. We could hurt you, but we take you as a brother into our hearts with love, good thoughts, and admiration.

Cassius. Your vote will be as important as any in giving out positions in the new government.

Brutus. Only be patient until we have calmed the people who are filled with fear, then we will tell you the reasons why I, who loved Caesar when I struck him, did this.

Antony. I believe you are wise. Let each man give me his bloody hand. First, Marcus Brutus, I will

---

[13] cut off—killed.

shake your hand. Next, Caius Cassius, I take your hand. Now, Decius Brutus, yours. Now yours, Metellus. Yours, Cinna, and my valiant Casca, yours. Though last, not least in love, yours, good Trebonius. Gentlemen all—alas, what shall I say? Because you know I was Caesar's friend, you must think I am either a coward or a flatterer. [Antony *speaks to* Caesar's *dead body.*] Caesar, I did love you. That is true. If your spirit looks on us now, shall it not make you sadder than your death to see your friend Antony next to your dead body. Does it pain you to see him shaking the bloody hands of the men who killed you, most noble Caesar? If I had as many eyes as you have wounds, and each one was crying as fast as your blood is flowing out of your body, it would look better than for me to be friends with your enemies. Pardon me, Julius! Here were you hunted down like a deer, here you fell, and here your hunters stand covered with your lifeblood like a sign of honor. O world, you were the forest for this hart,[14] and this man, O world, was your heart! How like a deer hit by many princes do you lie here, Caesar!

---

[14] hart—male deer. *Wordplay:* The words *hart* and *heart* sound the same.

Cassius. Mark Antony—

Antony. Pardon me, Caius Cassius. Caesar's enemies will say this. You can't expect a friend to say less.

Cassius. I don't blame you for praising Caesar. But what agreement do you plan on having with us? Will you be in the list of our friends, or shall we go on and not depend on you?

Antony. I shook your hands to show that I am your friend. But I could not think of friendship when I saw Caesar's body. I am your friend and love you all if you can give me good reasons why and how Caesar was dangerous to Rome.

Brutus. If we couldn't tell you why, then what you see here would be the work of savages. But, our reasons are so good that even if you were the son of Caesar, you would be satisfied.

Antony. That's all I want. I would like, also, to take his body to the marketplace and, as his friend, to speak to the people at his funeral.

Brutus. You shall, Mark Antony.

Cassius. Brutus, may I speak with you? [*Aside to* Brutus] You don't know what you're doing. Do not let him speak at Caesar's funeral. He will make the people pity Caesar.

Brutus. Pardon me. I will do this. But I will speak before Antony does and show the reasons for Caesar's death. I will tell everyone that we are letting Antony speak because we wish Caesar to have a proper funeral. It will help us more than hurt us.

Cassius. I don't know what will happen. I don't like it.

Brutus. [*Aside to* Mark Antony] Mark Antony, you may take Caesar's body. In your funeral speech, do not blame us, but speak all the good you can remember about Caesar. And say that you are doing it with our permission. If you don't do this, you will have no part in his funeral. I will speak in the same place before you speak.

Antony. I agree. I don't want anything else.

Brutus. Prepare Caesar's body then, and follow us.

[*Everyone exits but* Antony.]

Antony. [*To* Caesar's *dead body*[15]] O pardon me, you bleeding piece of earth, when I am **meek**[16] and gentle with these butchers. You are the ruins of the noblest man that ever lived. Sorrow will come to the hand that shed this costly blood! Standing here over your wounds, I will predict—your wounds open their mouths and beg me to speak—a curse shall fall on men. In all parts of Italy there will be war. Blood and destruction will be so normal, and dreadful sights will be so familiar, that mothers will just smile when they see their babies **quartered**.[17] All pity will be choked because people will be so used to evil acts. And Caesar's ghost will walk the earth hunting for revenge with the goddess of destruction, come hot from hell, by his side. Here, he will cry, "**Havoc**!"[18] and release the dogs of war. This stinking murder shall cause many to die, and heaven shall smell rotting dead men and hear many crying to die.

[*Enter Octavius's* Servant. *Octavius is Caesar's nephew and adopted son.*]

---

[15] This soliloquy is very famous.

[16] **meek**—patient, moderate.

[17] **quartered**—cut in four pieces.

[18] **Havoc**—destruction.

Antony. You serve Octavius Caesar, don't you?

Servant. I do, Mark Antony.

Antony. Caesar wrote asking Octavius to come to Rome.

Servant. Octavius got his letters, and is coming. He told me to say to you—[*The* Servant *sees Caesar's dead body.*] O Caesar!

Antony. Your heart is full of sorrow. Go somewhere and cry. Sorrow I see is catching, for seeing your tears, my eyes begin to water. Is your master coming?

Servant. He plans to stay within twenty-one miles of Rome tonight.

Antony. Go to him quickly! Tell him what has happened. Here is a sorrowful Rome, a dangerous Rome. It is not safe for Octavius to come here yet. Go quickly, and tell him. Yet, stay a while. Don't leave until you help me carry this body into the marketplace. There I shall see, when I give my speech, how the people will take the cruel actions of these bloody men. Then you can tell young Octavius what is happening. Help me.

[*They exit, carrying Caesar's body.*]

ACT THREE, SCENE TWO

In the Forum, Brutus speaks to the people about why Caesar's ambition was dangerous to Rome. The people cheer Brutus and want him to take Caesar's place. Then Antony speaks. He asks why, if Caesar was ambitious, he refused the crown three times. Antony wins the people to his side by reading Caesar's will, in which he leaves his wealth to the people. Antony calls Caesar's murderers "honorable men," but he encourages the people to hate them. The crowd rushes off to kill the murderers. Octavius has arrived in Rome, but Brutus and Cassius have fled.

[*Enter* Brutus *and* Cassius, *with a crowd of* Plebeians.[1]]

Plebeians. We will be satisfied; let us be satisfied![2]

Brutus. Then follow me, and listen to me, friends.
[*Aside to* Cassius] Cassius, go into the next

---

[1] Plebeians—a social class in Rome, the common people.

[2] The crowd is shouting. Shakespeare did not want everyone to say the same thing at the same time. He wanted to make it seem like a crowd near to rioting.

street and take some of this crowd with you. [*To the crowd*] Those who wish to hear me, stay here. Those who will listen to Cassius, go with him. We will explain why Caesar had to die.

First Plebeian. I will hear Brutus speak.

Second Plebeian. I will hear Cassius; then we can compare their reasons.

[Cassius *exits with some of the* Plebeians. Brutus *stands on a platform.*]

Third Plebeian. The noble Brutus is going to speak. Silence!

Brutus. Please, be patient and listen until I finish. Romans, countrymen, friends, hear me for the important news I have to give you, and be silent so you may hear. Believe me because I am honorable, and respect my honor so that you can believe me. Use your wisdom to judge if I am wrong. If there is anyone here who is a good friend of Caesar, I say to him that Brutus's love for Caesar was no less than his. If that friend asks why Brutus rose against Caesar, this is my answer: Not that I loved Caesar less, but that I loved Rome more. Would you rather have Caesar living and all die as slaves, or have Caesar dead and all live as free men? As much as Caesar loved me, I weep for him. As he was fortunate, I rejoice for him. As he was brave, I honor him. But, as he was ambitious, I killed him. There are tears for his love; joy for his fortune; honor for his bravery; and death for his ambition. Who is here so low that he would like to be a slave? If any of you, speak up, for you I have offended. Who is so savage that he would not be a Roman? If any of you, speak up, for you have I offended. Who is so evil that he will not love his country? If any of you, speak up, for you have I offended. I pause for a reply.[3]

All. None, Brutus, none.

Brutus. Then none have I offended. I have done no more to Caesar than you shall do to me if I become too ambitious. Caesar's life and death are recorded in the Capitol. His glory has not been taken away. Nor have his faults, for which he died, been made to seem worse.

[Mark Antony *and others enter with Caesar's body in a coffin.*]

---

[3] The long speeches by Brutus and Mark Antony in this scene are models of rhetorical skill. Rhetoric is the art of speaking or writing effectively, with persuasion.

Brutus. Here comes his body, **mourned**[4] by Mark Antony who, though he had no part in the death, shall receive the benefit of his dying, a voice in the government, as you all shall. With this I leave. As I killed my best friend for the good of Rome, I have the same dagger to use on myself when it shall please my country to need my death.

All. Live, Brutus, live, live!

First Plebeian. Carry him to his home in triumph.

Second Plebeian. Give him a statue like his ancestors have.

Third Plebeian. Let him be Caesar!

Fourth Plebeian. If we crown Brutus, it will be like crowning a better Caesar.

First Plebeian. We'll take him to his house with cheers.

Brutus. My countrymen—

Second Plebeian. Peace! Silence! Brutus speaks.

First Plebeian. Peace, listen!

Brutus. Good countrymen, let me leave alone. And for my sake, stay here with Antony. Honor

---

[4] **mourned**—sorrowed for.

Caesar's **corpse**,[5] and honor Antony's speech about the good that Caesar did, which Mark Antony, with our permission, is allowed to make. I beg you, let no one leave until Antony has spoken.

First Plebeian. Stay, listen, let us hear Mark Antony!

Third Plebeian. Let him stand on the platform. We'll hear him. Noble Antony, go up.

Antony. I thank Brutus for asking you all to stay.

[Antony *goes up to speak.*]

Fourth Plebeian. What did he say about Brutus?

Third Plebeian. He thanked Brutus.

Fourth Plebeian. He'd better not say anything bad about Brutus!

First Plebeian. Caesar was a tyrant.

Third Plebeian. He was worse than a tyrant. That's for sure. We are blessed that Rome is rid of him.

Second Plebeian. Peace! Let us hear what Antony says.

---

[5] **corpse**—dead body.

Antony. You noble Romans—

All. Peace. Listen. Let us hear him.

Antony.[6] Friends, Romans, countrymen, lend me your ears.
I come to bury Caesar, not to praise him.
The evil that men do lives after them;
The good is oft interred[7] with their bones.
So let it be with Caesar. The noble Brutus
Hath told you that Caesar was ambitious.
If it were so, it was a grievous[8] fault,
And grievously hath Caesar answered[9] it.
Here, under leave[10] of Brutus and the rest
(For Brutus is an honorable man,
So are they all, all honorable men)
Come I to speak in Caesar's funeral.
He was my friend, faithful and just to me;
But Brutus says he was ambitious,
And Brutus is an honorable man.

Caesar has brought many prisoners back to Rome whose wealth went to Rome, not to Caesar. Did this make Caesar seem ambitious? When the poor cried, Caesar wept. Ambition

---

[6] The next sixteen lines are in Shakespeare's original words. This is one of the most famous speeches in Shakespeare's writing.

[7] oft interred—often buried.

[8] grievous—very bad.

[9] answered—paid the penalty for.

[10] under leave—with permission.

should be made of stronger stuff. Yet Brutus says he was ambitious, and Brutus is an honorable man. You all saw that on the Lupercal, three times I tried to give him a kingly crown, which he three times turned down. Was this ambition? Yet Brutus says he was ambitious, and surely he is an honorable man. I don't speak to prove Brutus wrong, but here am I, to speak what I know. You all loved him once, and you had reasons. What reasons keep you from mourning for him now? O good judgment! You have stopped being men and turned into wild animals. Men have lost their good judgment! I cannot speak any more for a minute. My heart is in the coffin there with Caesar, and I must pause until it comes back to me.

First Plebeian. What he is saying makes a lot of sense.

Second Plebeian. If you think about it, Caesar was greatly wronged.

Third Plebeian. Was he? I am afraid someone worse will take his place.

Fourth Plebeian. Did you hear what Antony said? Caesar would not take a crown. Therefore, it is certain that he was not ambitious.

First Plebeian. If that's true, there will be people who will suffer for this murder.

Second Plebeian. [*Pointing at* Antony.] Poor soul, his eyes are as red as fire from weeping.

Third Plebeian. There's not a nobler man in Rome than Antony.

Fourth Plebeian. Now listen to him. He begins to speak.

Antony. Just yesterday Caesar's word would have been a command; now he lies there, and even the poorest do not bow down to him now. O masters, if I wanted to stir your hearts and minds to mutiny and rage, I should do Brutus wrong, and Cassius wrong, who, you all know, are honorable men. I will not do them wrong. I rather choose to wrong the dead, to wrong myself and you, than to wrong such honorable men. But here's a letter with Caesar's seal[11] on it. I found it in his study. It is his will. If the people heard what Caesar left them, which, pardon me, I don't mean to read, then they would go and kiss dead Caesar's wounds, and dip their handkerchiefs in his sacred blood. Yes,

---

[11] Caesar's seal—a stamp. Important letters and documents were sealed with hot wax. The person sending the letter stamped his personal seal into the hot wax.

they would beg for a hair off his head to remember him by, and when they die, they would leave it in their wills, giving it as a treasure to their children.

Fourth Plebeian. We'll hear the will; read it, Mark Antony.

All. The will, the will! We will hear Caesar's will.

Antony. Have patience, gentle friends. I must not read it. It is not right that you know how much Caesar loved you. You are not wood. You are not stones, but men. And being men, hearing Caesar's will, you will go mad with anger. It's good that you don't know that he left everything to you. For if you should know it, what would come of it?

Fourth Plebeian. Read the will! We'll hear it, Antony, you shall read us the will, Caesar's will!

Antony. Will you be patient? Will you wait a while? I said too much when I told you about the will. I am afraid I have wronged the honorable men whose daggers have stabbed Caesar. I do fear it.

Fourth Plebeian. They were traitors. They're not honorable men!

All. The will! The will!

Second Plebeian. They were villains, murderers! The will. Read the will!

Antony. You will make me read the will? Then make a ring around the corpse of Caesar, and let me show you the man who made the will. Can I come down? Will you let me?

Second Plebeian. Come down.

[Antony *leaves the platform.*]

Third Plebeian. We will let you.

Fourth Plebeian. A ring! Stand around him!

First Plebeian. Stand back! Stand away from the body!

Second Plebeian. Make room for Antony, most noble Antony!

Antony. Don't crowd in so close. Stand farther away!

All. Stand back. Move back!

Antony. If you have tears, get ready to shed them now. You all know this toga. I remember the first time that Caesar put it on. It was a summer evening, in his tent, on the day he conquered the Nervii.[12] [*Pointing to Caesar's wounds*] Look, Cassius' dagger ran through here. See what a tear the spiteful Casca made? Through this hole the well-beloved Brutus stabbed, and as he pulled out his cursed dagger, see how Caesar's blood followed it, as if his blood were rushing out to see if his friend Brutus had really knocked so unkindly on his door. For Brutus, as you know, was Caesar's favorite. Judge, O you gods, how dearly Caesar loved him! This was the unkindest cut of all. For when the noble Caesar saw him stab, ingratitude, stronger than the traitor's arms, defeated him. Then his mighty heart failed him. At the base of Pompey's statue, which was covered with his blood, great Caesar fell. O what a fall was there, my countrymen! Then I, and you, and all of us fell down, while bloody **treason**[13] triumphs over us. O now you weep, and I see you feel the effect of pity. These are kind tears. Gentle souls, do you weep when you see the wounds in our Caesar's clothes? [Antony *pulls away the toga that has been covering Caesar's body.*] Look here! Here he is himself, ruined, as you can see, by traitors.

---

[12] the Nervii—a very warlike group of people who almost beat the Romans. Their defeat was one of Caesar's great victories.

[13] **treason**—attempt to overthrow a country or government.

First Plebeian. O pitiful sight!

Second Plebeian. O noble Caesar!

Third Plebeian. O terrible day!

Fourth Plebeian. O traitors, villains!

First Plebeian. O most bloody sight!

All of the Plebeians. We will have revenge! Revenge! Hunt for those traitors everywhere! Burn, fire, kill, kill! Don't let a single traitor live!

Antony. Stop, countrymen!

First Plebeian. Quiet! Hear the noble Antony.

Second Plebeian. We'll hear him! We'll follow him! We'll die with him!

Antony. Good friends, sweet friends, don't let me stir you to a sudden flood of **mutiny**.[14] The men who have done this deed are honorable. What personal reasons they had for hating Caesar and murdering him, alas, I don't know. They are wise and honorable, and will, no doubt, give you good reasons for what they did. I don't come here, friends, to steal your hearts away. I am no trained public speaker, as Brutus is. You all know me as a man who speaks the

---

[14] **mutiny**—revolt against authority.

plain truth and who was Caesar's friend. Those who permitted me to speak here know I am not clever. I don't have big words, or a speaker's gestures, or reputation, or clever sayings, or the training in speech to make men angry. I just say what I really think and feel. I have told you what you already knew. I show you sweet Caesar's wounds, poor, silent mouths that ask for your pity. I ask these wounds to speak for me. But if I were Brutus, and Brutus were Antony, then there would be an Antony who would put a voice in every wound of Caesar that would cause the stones of Rome to rise and mutiny.

All. We'll mutiny.

First Plebeian. We'll burn Brutus's house.

Third Plebeian. Let's go! Find the murderers!

Antony. Wait. Hear me, countrymen, hear me speak.

All. Quiet, everyone! Hear Antony, most noble Antony!

Antony. Why, friends, you don't know what you are going to do. Why does Caesar deserve your love? Alas, you don't know. I must tell you then; you have forgotten the will I told you about.

All. Most true! The will. Let's stay and hear the will!

Antony. Here is the will, and marked with Caesar's seal. Caesar gives to every Roman citizen, to each man, seventy-five drachmas.[15]

Second Plebeian. Most noble Caesar! We'll **avenge**[16] his death!

Third Plebeian. O nobly generous Caesar!

Antony. There is more.

All. Quiet! Listen!

Antony. Also, he has left you all his gardens, summer houses, and orchards on this side of the Tiber. He has left them to you and to your children and to their children forever. They will be public parks for all of you to walk in and enjoy yourselves. Here was a great ruler! When will there be another like him?

First Plebeian. Never, never! Come, let's go! We'll burn his body in the holy place, and with torches lit on his funeral fire, we'll burn

---

[15] drachmas—silver coins.

[16] **avenge**—seek revenge for.

the traitors' houses. Carry Caesar's body to the Forum.

Second Plebeian. Go, fetch fire!

Third Plebeian. Break some benches for wood.

Fourth Plebeian. Pull apart anything made of wood, anything!

[*The crowd of* Plebeians *exits, carrying Caesar's body.*]

Antony. Now let it work: Mischief, you have begun. Do what you will!

[*Enter a* Servant.]

Antony. What do you want?

Servant. Sir, Octavius is already in Rome.

Antony. Where is he?

Servant. He and Lepidus are at Caesar's house.

Antony. I will go there at once to meet him. I wanted him to come. The goddess of fortune is happy with us and will give us anything.

Servant. I heard him say that Brutus and Cassius have ridden like madmen through the gates of Rome.

Antony. Perhaps they heard how the people were moved by my words. Take me to Octavius.

[Antony *and the* Servant *exit.*]

ACT THREE, SCENE THREE

On a street, the rioting crowd kills a poet who has the same name as Cinna, one of Caesar's murderers. The crowd is out of control.

[*Enter* Cinna *the poet.*]

Cinna. I dreamed last night that I feasted with Caesar. I have a very bad feeling about this. I don't want to be out here, but something forces me to be here.

[*Enter* Plebeians.]

First Plebeian. What is your name?

Second Plebeian. Where are you going?

Third Plebeian. Where do you live?

Fourth Plebeian. Are you a married man, or a bachelor?

Second Plebeian. Answer every man at once.

First Plebeian. Yes, and briefly.

Fourth Plebeian. Yes, and wisely.

Third Plebeian. Yes, and tell the truth, or it will go badly for you.

Cinna. [*He does not, at first, realize the danger he is in. He starts out joking.*] What is my name? Where am I going? Where do I live? Am I married or a bachelor? Then to answer every man quickly and briefly, wisely and truly: wisely I say, I am a bachelor.

Second Plebeian. That's like saying that married men are fools. I'll give you a good blow for saying that. Go on, quickly.

Cinna. Quickly, I am going to Caesar's funeral.

First Plebeian. As a friend or an enemy?

Cinna. As a friend.

Second Plebeian. That is a quick answer.

Fourth Plebeian. Briefly, where do you live?

Cinna. Briefly, I live by the Capitol.

Third Plebeian. Tell us your name, truly.

Cinna. Truly, my name is Cinna.

First Plebeian. Tear him to pieces; he's a murderer.

Cinna. I am Cinna the poet; I am Cinna the poet!

Fourth Plebeian. Tear him apart for his bad poetry. Tear him for his bad poetry.

Cinna. I am not Cinna the murderer.

Fourth Plebeian. It doesn't matter. His name's Cinna. Pull his name out of his heart and let him go.

Third Plebeian. Tear him to pieces, tear him! [*The mob attacks* Cinna.] Come, get torches![1] Burn! To Brutus's house, to Cassius's, burn them all! Some go to Decius's house, and some to Casca's; some go to Ligarius's! Away, go!

[*The crowd of* Plebeians *exits, shouting, with* Cinna.]

---

[1] torches—lights made of sticks of burning wood.

act four

ACT FOUR, SCENE ONE

In Antony's house in Rome, he and Octavius and Lepidus (all three now called the Triumvirate) decide which Romans shall live and which shall be killed. When Lepidus goes to get Caesar's will, Antony tells Octavius that Lepidus is a weak leader and suggests they get rid of him. They begin to discuss how to defeat Brutus and Cassius.

[Antony, Octavius, *and* Lepidus *are seated at a table.*]

Antony. These men must die. I have marked their name on the list.

Octavius. Your brother must die, too. Do you agree to that, Lepidus?

Lepidus. I agree.

Octavius. Check his name on the list, Antony.

Lepidus. I will agree that my brother will not live, if you agree that your sister's son Publius shall not live, Mark Antony.

Antony. He shall not live. Look, with a mark I sentence him to death. But, Lepidus, go to Caesar's house: bring Caesar's will here, and we shall decide how to keep some of what Caesar gave away.

Lepidus. What? Will you be here when I come back?

Octavius. Here, or at the Capitol.

[Lepidus *exits.*]

Antony. Lepidus is a small man who has done nothing. He's only good to send on errands. Do you think it is right that the Roman empire should be divided into three parts and he should get one of them?

Octavius. You thought him fit to rule. You took his vote on who should live and die on our list of those to die.

Antony. Octavius, I have lived longer than you and know what we should do. Although we will give honors to Lepidus so that he takes some of the blame for what we must do, he shall carry his honors like an ass bears gold. He will grunt and sweat under the hard work, and will be led or driven as we wish. When he does what we wish with the treasure, then we will unload him and turn him out into the common field like an ass without a load. He will shake his ears and live as an ass lives.

Octavius. You may do as you wish, but he's a good and brave soldier.

Antony. So is my horse, Octavius, and, for that, I make sure he is taken care of. My horse is an animal that I have taught to fight, to turn, to stop, to run. He does what I tell him to do, and in some ways that's what Lepidus is like. He must be taught and trained and told what to do. He has no thoughts of his own. He thinks ideas are new that other men have finished with and thrown away. Don't talk of him as anything but a tool. And now, Octavius, listen to what matters. Brutus and Cassius are raising an army. We must face them right away. So, let's combine our forces. Let's get the help of our friends, collect all the money we can, and decide what we must tell the people and what dangers we must keep secret.

Octavius. Let us get ready, for we are like captured bears tied to a stake and surrounded by dogs who wish to kill us. Some people who smile at us, I fear, in their hearts wish to hurt us.

[*They exit.*]

ACT FOUR, SCENE TWO

In front of Brutus's army tent outside the city of Sardis, Lucilius tells Brutus that Cassius is coming. Cassius seems changed. When he arrives, they go into Brutus's tent to talk about their disagreements.

[Brutus, *his friend* Lucilius, *and other* Soldiers *enter.* Titinius *and* Pindarus, *from Cassius's army, meet them.*]

Brutus. [*Speaking to* Lucilius.] Halt!

Lucilius. [*Turning to give the order to the* Soldiers.] Halt!

Brutus. What now, Lucilius? Is Cassius near?

Lucilius. He is near, and Pindarus has come to bring you greetings from his master.

Brutus. I am glad to get his greetings. [*To* Pindarus] Your master is near. Maybe he can explain some things to me.

Pindarus. My noble master is an honorable man whom all respect.

Brutus. I don't doubt that. [*Aside to* Lucilius] Tell me, Lucilius, how did he treat you?

Lucilius. He treated me with courtesy and respect but was not as friendly as he used to be.

Brutus. You are describing a hot friend cooling. When friendship begins to sicken and decay, the old friend becomes too nice. Not so in real friendship. False friends are like horses that seem eager to go into battle. [*A distant sound of marching keeps getting nearer.*] At first, they look brave and ready to fight. But when they feel the bloody spur, they lower their heads and, like old, worn-out horses, fail when they are tested. Is Cassius's army coming?

Lucilius. They will stay overnight in Sardis. Most of his army are with him here.

[*The sound of an army stopping.*]

Brutus. Listen, he is here. Let's go slowly to meet him.

[*Enter* Cassius *and his immediate staff.*]

Cassius. [*To the* Soldiers] Halt!

Brutus. [*To his* Soldiers] Halt! Give the command.

First Soldier. Halt!

Second Soldier. Halt!

Third Soldier. Halt!

Cassius. [*To* Brutus] Most noble brother, you have treated me unfairly.

Brutus. Judge me, you gods. I treat my enemies fairly. Why would I treat my brother unfairly?

Cassius. Brutus, this reasonable look of yours hides the wrongs you do me.

Brutus. Cassius, keep calm and speak quietly about your problems. Do not let our armies see us argue. They should see only friendship between us. Tell your men to move away a little. Then, in my tent, Cassius, tell me your problems, and I will listen to you carefully.

Cassius. Pindarus, tell our commanders to lead the men a short distance away from here.

Brutus. Lucilius, you do the same. Don't let anyone come to our tent until we have finished talking. Let Lucius and Titinius guard our door.

[*They exit.*]

ACT FOUR, SCENE THREE

In Brutus's tent, Cassius and Brutus argue angrily. When Brutus accuses Cassius of bringing dishonor on their cause, Cassius offers to let Brutus kill him. The two men calm down. Brutus then tells Cassius that Portia has killed herself. Other officers arrive bringing news of the approaching armies. Brutus tells Cassius that their forces should meet the enemy at Philippi. Cassius finally agrees. As Brutus gets ready for bed, the ghost of Caesar appears and promises to see him again at Philippi.

[*Enter* Brutus *and* Cassius.]

Cassius. I'll tell you how you wronged me. You judged my man Lucius Pella and found him guilty of taking bribes here from the Sardinians. When I wrote letters asking for him to be let go because he was my friend, you ignored them.

Brutus. You shouldn't have written letters asking for him to be set free.

Cassius. In times like these, it isn't right to punish every little wrong action.

Brutus. Let me tell you, Cassius, people are saying that you yourself are greedy and sell government jobs to people who have no skills or knowledge.

Cassius. I . . . I am greedy? You know that if anyone but you, Brutus, said that, it would be his last words!

Brutus. Your good name protects you from punishment.

Cassius. Punishment?

Brutus. Remember March, remember the Ides of March. Didn't great Caesar bleed for the sake of justice? Was there some villain who stabbed him and didn't do it for justice? What, shall one of us, that struck the greatest man in this world, now dirty his fingers with low bribes and sell our important positions for a little filthy money? I had rather be a dog and howl at the moon than to be such a Roman.

Cassius. Brutus, do not anger me more. I won't take it. You forget who you are when you try to tell me what to do. I am a soldier. I am a more experienced soldier than you, and I am better able to decide what should be done than you.

Brutus. That's not true. You are not, Cassius.

Cassius. I am.

Brutus. I say you are not.

Cassius. Don't argue with me any more. I shall forget myself.[1] Think about your own safety. Don't make me more angry.

Brutus. Get away from me, small man!

Cassius. Is it possible?

Brutus. Hear me, for I will speak. Must I listen to your anger and agree with it? Shall I be frightened by the crazy looks of a madman?

Cassius. O you gods, you gods, must I put up with all this?

Brutus. All this? Yes, and more. Be angry until your proud heart breaks. Go show your *slaves* how angry you can be, make them tremble. Must *I* pay attention? Must *I* listen to you? Must *I* stop and bow down to your bad temper? By the gods, you shall swallow the poison of your

---

[1] I will forget you are my friend and hurt you.

anger even if it kills you. For, from this day on, I'll use you for amusement, yes, to laugh at, when you are angry.

Cassius. Has it come to this?

Brutus. You say you are a better soldier. Show me how. Let me see how your bragging is true, and I shall be very pleased. For my own part, I shall be glad to learn how to be a soldier from such a noble man.

Cassius. You wrong me every way. You wrong me, Brutus. I said I was a more experienced soldier, not a better soldier. Did I say better?

Brutus. If you did, I don't care.

Cassius. When Caesar lived, he dared not make me this angry.

Brutus. Be quiet! You didn't dare tempt him to make you angry.

Cassius. I didn't dare?

Brutus. No.

Cassius. What? I dared not tempt him?

Brutus. For fear of your life, you dared not tempt Caesar.

Cassius. Don't rely too much on our friendship. I may do something that I shall be sorry for.

Brutus. You have done that which you should be sorry for. There is no terror in your threats, Cassius. I am protected by honesty. Your threats go by me like wind. I am not bothered by them. I asked you to send money. You didn't. I can't raise money by evil ways.[2] By heaven, I had rather cut open my heart and let my blood drops be coins than cheat the poor people out of their filthy pennies. I asked you to send money to help me pay my soldiers. You wouldn't. Was that what Cassius would have done in the past? Would I have denied you money if you needed it? When I grow so greedy that I keep such filthy money from my friends, be ready, gods, with all your thunderbolts.[3] Dash me to pieces!

Cassius. I didn't refuse you.

Brutus. You did.

Cassius. I did not. Whoever brought that answer to you was a fool. You have broken my heart. A good friend would forgive my faults, but you make my faults bigger than they really are.

---

[2] Brutus won't raise money in immoral ways, but he will take money from Cassius that Cassius has obtained in immoral ways.

[3] thunderbolts—lightning.

Brutus. I did not, until you used them to trick me.

Cassius. You hate me.

Brutus. I do not like your faults.

Cassius. A friendly eye would not see my faults.

Brutus. A flatterer's eye would not see those faults, even if they look as big as the highest mountain.

Cassius. Come, Antony. And young Octavius, come! Revenge yourself on me alone, for I am tired of this world, hated by my friend, defied by my brother, scolded like a slave. All my faults are written in a notebook, studied, memorized so they can be thrown in my face. O, I could cry until my spirit wept out of me and I died. There is my dagger. And here is my chest: inside is my heart. To me it is more valuable than gold, than all the gold in all the world. If you are a Roman, cut out my heart. I, who didn't give you gold, will give you my heart. Strike me as you struck Caesar. For I know that when you hated him the most, you loved him better than you ever loved me.

Brutus. Put your dagger away. Be angry when you want to be. You shall be free to be angry. Do what you want. When you insult me, I shall just blame your anger. O Cassius, you are partnered with a lamb who carries anger as a flint[4] carries fire. If you strike me often, I will finally give a spark, but right away I am cold again.

Cassius. Have I lived to be just a joke to Brutus when he is upset or in a bad mood?

Brutus. When I said that, I was angry, too.

Cassius. Are you willing to admit that? Give me your hand.

Brutus. And my heart too.

Cassius. O Brutus!

Brutus. What's wrong?

Cassius. Aren't you enough my friend to put up with me when that bad temper that I got from my mother makes me forget how I should act?

Brutus. Yes, Cassius, and from now on, when you get too angry, I'll think it's the temper from your mother and leave it at that.

[*Voices are heard offstage.*]

---

[4] flint—a stone that sparks when hit against steel. Flint and steel can be used to start a fire.

Poet. [*Offstage*] Let me in to see the generals. There is some problem between them. It's not right they should be left alone.

Lucilius. [*Offstage*] You shall not go in.

Poet. [*Offstage*] Nothing but death will stop me.

[*Enter a* Poet, *followed by* Lucilius, Titinius, *and* Lucius.][5]

Cassius. What's this? What's the matter?

Poet. For shame, you generals. What do you mean?
Be friends, as two such men should be.
I know because I've seen more years, I'm sure,
than ye.[6]

Cassius. [*Laughing*] How badly does this dog rhyme!

Brutus. Get out of here, sirrah: disrespectful fellow, get away.

Cassius. Don't be angry with him. It's just the way he is.

Brutus. I'll learn not to be angry with him when he learns when he shouldn't make jokes. What

---

[5] This very short section with the poet is mentioned in Shakespeare's historical source, Plutarch.

[6] ye—you.

good are these rhyming fools[7] in war? Clown, get out of here.

Cassius. Away, get away! Be gone!

[*The* Poet *exits.*]

Brutus. Lucilius and Titinius, tell the commanders to set up camp for the night.

Cassius. And return bringing Messala with you right away.

[Lucilius *and* Titinius *exit.*]

Brutus. Lucius, bring us a bowl of wine.

[Lucius *exits.*]

Cassius. I did not think you could have been so angry.

Brutus. O Cassius, I am sick with grief.

Cassius. You don't use your philosophy[8] if you let yourself be troubled by accidents.

Brutus. No man deals with sorrow better than I do. Portia is dead!

Cassius. What? Portia?

---

[7] rhyming fools—poets. Remember, Shakespeare was a poet.

[8] philosophy—plan for living life. Brutus was a Stoic. In the Stoic philosophy everything that happened, good or bad, was supposed to be treated equally. A Stoic should not care what happened, nor be very happy nor very sad.

Brutus. She is dead.

Cassius. How did I escape from being killed by you when we argued? O how can you take such a terrible loss? What caused her death?

Brutus. She couldn't stand my being away from her, and she was saddened that young Octavius and Mark Antony have become so strong—the news of their power came to me with the news of her death—so she went mad. When her servants were gone, she swallowed hot coals from the fire.

Cassius. And died that way?

Brutus. That's right.

Cassius. O you immortal gods!

[*Enter* Lucius *with wine and candles.*]

Brutus. Don't talk about her any more. Give me a glass of wine, Lucius. In this wine I bury all unkindness, Cassius.

[Brutus *drinks.*]

Cassius. My heart is thirsty for that noble promise. Fill my cup, Lucius, until the wine runs over. I cannot drink too much of your friendship.

[Cassius *drinks.* Lucius *exits.*]

[*Enter* Titinius *and* Messala.]

Brutus. Come in, Titinius! Welcome, good Messala. Now sit close around the candle, and let us talk about what we have to do.

Cassius. [*Almost to himself*] Portia, are you gone?

Brutus. [*To* Cassius] No more about that, I beg you. [*To the other men*] Messala, I have received letters that say young Octavius and Mark Antony are coming quickly to attack us with a large army. They are headed toward Philippi.

Messala. They got the money to pay for their soldiers by calling people traitors, killing them, and taking over their money and property. Octavius, Antony, and Lepidus have put to death a hundred senators.

Brutus. This does not agree with the news I received. My letters say seventy senators were killed, Cicero being one of them.

Cassius. Cicero was killed?

Messala. Cicero is dead, and by the order of the Triumvirate. Did you get your wife's letters, my lord?[9]

---

[9] Some Shakespearean students think this section where Brutus is getting the news of his dead wife for the second time was an earlier version and was accidentally left in. It might also be that Brutus, who always likes to look noble, is trying to impress his men with how he can take bad news.

Brutus. No, Messala.

Messala. Did you get any news about her in your letters?

Brutus. Nothing, Messala.

Messala. I think that is very strange.

Brutus. Why do you ask? Did you hear something about her?

Messala. No, my lord.

Brutus. Now, as you are a Roman, tell me the truth.

Messala. Then, like a Roman, bear the truth I tell. She is dead, and in a strange manner.

Brutus. Why, farewell, Portia. We all must die, Messala. By thinking that Portia had to die for some time, I have learned to conquer the pain of her death.

Messala. This is the way great men should meet great losses.

Cassius. I can take as much pain as you in theory, but I could not stand this so easily.

Brutus. Well, we are alive and must work! What do you think of meeting the enemy at Philippi?

Cassius. I don't think it's a good idea.

Brutus. Your reason?

Cassius. It's better that the enemy comes to us. That way the enemy will use up his food and supplies, tire his soldiers, hurting himself, while we, lying still, are rested, protected, and ready to strike.

Brutus. Good reasons must be overcome by better reasons. We have forced the people between here and Philippi to give us food and men. Those people are no longer our friends. If Antony and Octavius come through their land, they will be given supplies, encouragement, and men to help beat us. We must stop that from happening. If we meet the enemy at Philippi, these people will not be able to help Antony and Octavius.

Cassius. Listen to me, good brother.

Brutus. Excuse me. You must also remember that we have had all the help we can get from our friends. Our army is as large as it's going to get. The enemy army gets larger every day. We are at the top of our power, and we will only get weaker.

There is a tide in the affairs of men,
Which, taken at the flood, leads on to fortune;
Omitted, all the voyage of their life
Is bound in shallows and in miseries.
On such a full sea are we now afloat,
And we must take the current when it serves
Or lose our ventures.[10]

Cassius. Then, as you wish, go on: we will go ourselves and meet our enemies at Philippi.

Brutus. It has got late while we talked. We must sleep, but we won't sleep long. Is there anything else we need to talk about?

Cassius. No more. Good night. We will get up early tomorrow and leave.

[*Enter* Lucius.]

Brutus. Lucius, I am going to bed; farewell, good Messala.

[Lucius *exits.*]

Brutus. Good night, Titinius. Noble, noble Cassius, good night, and sleep well.

---

[10] These seven lines are in Shakespeare's original words. Men must take their opportunities when they arrive or not succeed.

Cassius. O my dear brother, this night started badly. Never let our souls be so divided from each other again! Let it not happen, Brutus.

Brutus. Everything is well.

Cassius. Good night, my lord.

Brutus. Good night, my brother.

Titinius and Messala. Good night, lord Brutus.

Brutus. Farewell, everyone.

[Cassius, Titinius, *and* Messala *exit.*]

[Lucius *enters with Brutus's robe.*]

Brutus. Give me the clothes. Where is your musical instrument?

Lucius. Here, in the tent.

Brutus. What, are you sleepy? Poor boy, I don't blame you. You have stayed up too late. Call Claudius and some of my other men. I'll have them sleep more comfortably here in my tent.

Lucius. [*Calling offstage*] Varro and Claudius!

[Varro *and* Claudius *enter.*]

Varro. Did you call, my lord?

Brutus. I want you, sirs, to sleep here in my tent tonight. I may need you to take a message later to my brother Cassius.

Varro. If you need us, we will stay awake until then.

Brutus. I will not have it so. Lie down, good sirs. I may change my mind. Look, Lucius, here's the book I was hunting for; I put it in the pocket of my robe.

[Varro *and* Claudius *lie down.*]

Lucius. I was sure your lordship didn't give it to me.

Brutus. You'll have to put up with me, good boy. I am very forgetful. Can you stay awake a little while and play some music?

Lucius. Yes, my lord, if it pleases you.

Brutus. It does, my boy. I cause you a lot of trouble, but you are good about it.

Lucius. It is my duty, sir.

Brutus. I should not ask you to do more than you can. I know young boys need sleep.

Lucius. I already slept, my lord.

Brutus. That's good, and you will sleep again. I will not keep you long. If I live, I will be good to you.

[Lucius *plays and sings, but soon falls asleep.*]

Brutus. This song makes me feel sleepy. O death-like sleep, do you lay like a lead mace[11] on my young musician? Gentle boy, good night. I will not wrong you by waking you up. If your head nods, you will break your instrument. I'll take it from you, and, good boy, good night. [Brutus *takes the boy's musical instrument and puts it in a safe place.*] Let me see, let me see. Didn't I turn down the corner of a page where I stopped reading? Here it is, I think.

[Brutus *sits. Caesar's* Ghost *enters.*]

Brutus. How poorly the candle burns. [Brutus *sees the* Ghost.] Ha! Who comes here? I think it is the weakness of my eyes that makes me see this monstrous thing. It comes toward me. Are you anything? Are you some god, some angel, or some devil? You make my blood run cold and my hair stand on end. Speak to me. What are you?

---

[11] mace—both a weapon and a staff of office. When a man was arrested, he was touched on the shoulder with the mace.

Ghost. Your evil spirit, Brutus!

Brutus. Why have you come here?

Ghost. I have come to tell you that you will see me at Philippi.

Brutus. Well, then I shall see you again?

Ghost. Yes, at Philippi.

Brutus. Why, I will see you at Philippi then.

[*The* Ghost *exits.*]

Brutus. Now that I have gathered my courage, you vanish. Evil spirit, I wish to talk with you some more. Boy! Lucius! Varro! Claudius! Sirs! awake! Claudius!

Lucius. [*He is still half asleep.*] The strings, my lord, are not in tune.

Brutus. He thinks he is still playing his instrument. Lucius, awake!

Lucius. My lord!

Brutus. Did your dream make you cry out, Lucius?

Lucius. My lord, I didn't know that I cried out.

Brutus. Yes, you did. Did you see anything?

Lucius. Nothing, my lord.

Brutus. Go back to sleep, Lucius. Claudius, fellow! You! Wake up!

Varro. My lord?

Claudius. My lord?

Brutus. Why did you cry out in your sleep, sirs?

Both. Did we, my lord?

Brutus. Yes. Did you see anything?

Varro. No, my lord. I saw nothing.

Claudius. Nor I, my lord.

Brutus. Go, and greet my brother Cassius. Tell him to let his army leave before mine. We will follow.

Both. It shall be done, my lord.

[*All exit.*]

act five

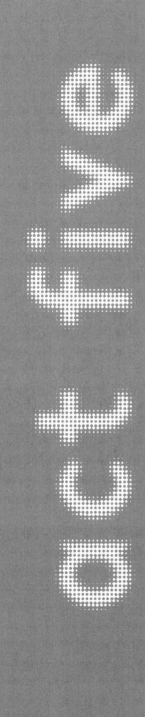

ACT FIVE, SCENE ONE

On the plains of Philippi, the four generals meet and exchange insults. Octavius and Antony leave. Cassius tells one of his officers he is afraid the battle will go badly for Brutus and himself. Finally, Brutus and Cassius say goodbye to each other in case they should die in battle.

[Octavius, Antony, *and their* Soldiers[1] *enter.*]

Octavius. See, Antony, what you predicted has come true.[2] You said the enemy would stay in the hills. It is not so. Their armies are going to meet us here. They mean to fight at Philippi, meeting us before we force them to fight.

Antony. It's nothing, I can see into their hearts. I know why they are doing this. They would be

[1] The armies must be suggested by a few soldiers, drums, flags, and noise offstage.

[2] Octavius is making fun of Antony. Antony believed that Brutus's and Cassius's armies would not meet them at Philippi, but would stay in the hills.

happy to be somewhere else. But they are meeting us here to persuade us that they will win; but it's not true.

[*A* Messenger *enters.*]

Messenger. Get ready, generals. The enemy comes on bravely. Their red flag of war is hung out. It is time to fight.

Antony. Octavius, lead your troops slowly onto the left-hand side of that flat field.

Octavius. I will lead them on to the right side; you go on to the left side.

Antony. Why do you go against me when we must make a quick decision?

Octavius. I don't go against you, but I will go on the right side.

[*The* Soldiers *march off.*]

[*Drum.* Brutus, Cassius, *and their* Soldiers, Lucilius, Titinius, Messala, *and others enter.*]

Brutus. They have stopped and wish to speak with us.[3]

---

[3] It was normal for enemy generals to meet and talk before a battle. This was a last chance to avoid the battle.

Cassius. Halt, Titinius; we must meet them between the two armies and talk.

[*At first* Octavius *and* Antony *would be on the opposite side of the stage from* Brutus *and* Cassius, *then the four would meet in the center.*]

Octavius. Mark Antony, shall we attack?

Antony. No, Caesar,[4] we will attack when they do. Let us go forward. The generals wish to speak to us.

Octavius. [*To* Lucilius] Do not attack until I give the signal.

Brutus. [*To* Antony *and* Octavius] Words before fighting? That's the way to do it, countrymen.

Octavius. Not that we love words better, as you do.

Brutus. Good words are better than bad strokes, Octavius.[5]

Antony. With your kind of bad strokes, Brutus, you give good words; just look at the hole you made in Caesar's heart, while you said "Long live Caesar!"

---

[4] Octavius, historically, was Caesar's adopted son, and after Caesar's death Octavius legally changed his name to Caesar.

[5] Words are better than fighting, also words are better than the marks you made on the list of people to be killed.

Cassius. Antony, we don't know how well you will fight. But your words rob the bees and leave them without honey.[6]

Antony. I have also stolen their sting.

Brutus. O yes, and the bees are soundless too, for you have stolen their buzzing,[7] Antony. You very wisely threaten before you sting.

Antony. Villains, you did not threaten before your wicked daggers hacked into the sides of Caesar. You smiled like apes, and fawned[8] like dogs, and bowed like slaves, kissing Caesar's feet while damned Casca, like a street dog, sneaked up behind and struck Caesar on the neck. O you flatterers!

Cassius. Flatterers? Now, Brutus, thank yourself! Antony would not have insulted us today, if you had done what Cassius asked.[9]

Octavius. Come, come, let's get to the battle. If arguing makes us sweat, then deciding the argument in battle will make us sweat redder drops. Look, I draw my sword against

---

[6] Cassius is talking about the words that Antony used to win the crowd at Caesar's funeral.

[7] buzzing—gossiping.

[8] fawned—acted humbly.

[9] Cassius reminds Brutus that Antony should have been killed when Caesar was killed.

murderers. When do you think I will put my sword away? Never, until Caesar's thirty-three wounds have been **avenged,**[10] or until another Caesar is killed by the sword of traitors.

Brutus. Caesar, you cannot die by traitors' hands unless you bring them with you.

Octavius. So I hope. I was not born to die on Brutus's sword.

Brutus. O, if you were the noblest of your family, young man, you could not die more honorably.

Cassius. He is a childish schoolboy, not worthy to die on your sword, and he is joined by Antony who spends his time at dances and wild parties.

Antony. You are still the same old Cassius!

Octavius. Come, Antony, let's go! We are ready for the fight, traitors! If you dare fight today, come to the battlefield; if not, come when you have found the courage.

[Octavius, Antony, *and their* Soldiers *exit.*]

Cassius. Well now, let the wind blow, the waves rise, and the ship toss. The storm has come, and no one knows what will happen.

---

[10] **avenged**—taken vengeance for, punished.

Brutus. Lucilius, come here, I need to speak to you!

Lucilius. My lord?

[Lucilius *and* Brutus *step to the side to talk.*]

Cassius. Messala!

Messala. [*Stepping near to* Cassius] What says my general?

Cassius. [*An aside between* Cassius *and* Messala.] Messala, this is my birthday. This very day was I born. Be my witness, Messala, that against my will, as it was against Pompey's,[11] I am forced to decide our future in this one battle. You know that I do not believe in signs that tell the future. Now I change my mind a little and believe some of these signs. As we came from Sardis, two mighty eagles landed on our front **ensign**,[12] and there they sat. They ate food out of our soldiers' hands and stayed with us to Philippi. This morning they flew away. In their place, ravens, crows, and other birds that feed on dead bodies fly over our heads and look down on us as if we were ready to die and become their food. Their shadows seem a deathly

---

[11] Pompey had not wanted to fight Caesar, but his generals talked him into it, and he was defeated.

[12] **ensign**—military sign or flag carried by troops as their symbol.

canopy[13] under which our army lies, ready to give up the ghost.[14]

Messala. Don't believe that.

Cassius. I only partly believe it. I will be cheerful and meet all danger without fear.

[Brutus *returns from speaking to* Lucilius.]

Brutus. That's right, Lucilius.

Cassius. Now, most noble Brutus, the gods are our friends, so we who love peace will live to old age! But since what men do is uncertain, let's think about the worst that can happen. If we lose this battle, this will be the last time that we speak together. If we lose, what will you do?

Brutus. I will continue to live by the Stoic philosophy that a man should be calm in defeat. I was unhappy with Cato when he killed himself after being defeated by Caesar. I don't know why, but I find it cowardly and sinful for a person to kill himself because he fears what might happen. I will make myself strong and accept what the gods who rule this earth have planned for me.

---

[13] **canopy**—overhanging shelter.

[14] give up the ghost—die.

Cassius. Then, if we lose this battle, you will be content to be led through the streets of Rome as a prisoner of war?

Brutus. No, Cassius, no. Don't think, you noble Roman, that Brutus will ever go to Rome in chains. My mind is too great. But today must end the work that the Ides of March began. I do not know if we shall meet again: therefore, let us take our everlasting farewell. Forever, and forever, farewell, Cassius! If we meet again, why, we shall smile; if not, why then, we made a good parting.

Cassius. Forever, and forever, farewell, Brutus. If we do meet again, we'll smile indeed. If not, it's true, this was a good parting.

Brutus. Why then, lead on. O that a man might know how a day would end before it ended. But it is enough that the day will end, and then the end is known. Come, let's go!

[*All exit.*]

ACT FIVE, SCENE TWO

On the battlefield, Brutus sends Messala to tell the army to attack.

[*The trumpets sound the signal to start the battle.* Brutus *and* Messala *enter.*]

Brutus. Ride, ride, Messala, take these orders to the commanders on the far side.

[*Loud trumpet calls.*]

Brutus. Let them attack at once, for I see that Octavius's men do not have much confidence in him. A sudden attack will make them run. Ride, ride, Messala! Let them all attack.

[Brutus *and* Messala *exit.*]

ACT FIVE, SCENE THREE

In another part of the battlefield, Antony's men have surrounded Cassius's army. Cassius thinks they have lost and that Titinius has been captured. Completely discouraged, he asks Pindarus to kill him. Titinius returns and, finding Cassius dead, kills himself. Brutus arrives from defeating Octavius's army. He mourns the deaths and prepares to attack again.

[*Trumpets.* Cassius *and* Titinius *enter.*]

Cassius. O, look, Titinius, look! Our cowardly men turn and run away! I have fought against my own men. Our own flag bearer was turning back. I killed the coward and took the flag from him.

Titinius. O Cassius, Brutus gave the order to attack too early. He had some advantage over Octavius and took it too eagerly. We are surrounded by Antony's men, but Brutus's soldiers are looting and do not see we need help.

[Pindarus *enters.*]

Pindarus. Get further away, my lord. Get further away! Mark Antony is in your camp, my lord. Get further away, noble Cassius, hurry!

Cassius. This hill is far enough. Look, look, Titinius! Are my tents on fire?

Titinius. They are, my lord.

Cassius. Titinius, if you are my friend, get on my horse and use your spurs on him until he has brought you to those troops over there. Come back and tell me if they are friends or enemies.

Titinius. I will be back quickly.

[Titinius *exits.*]

Cassius. Go, Pindarus, get higher on that hill. I have never been able to see very well. Keep your eye on Titinius. Tell me what you see.

[Pindarus *exits.*]

Pindarus. [*From above*[1]] O, my lord!

Cassius. What news?

Pindarus. Titinius is surrounded by soldiers on horseback. They are speeding toward him. He

---

[1] *From above*—from the stage balcony.

goes on. Now they almost have him! Now they are with him. Now some of them jump off their horses. O, he jumps off too. He's captured. [*Shouting heard offstage.*] And listen, they shout for joy.

Cassius. Come down; don't look any longer! O coward that I am, to live so long to see my best friend captured in front of me.

[Pindarus *comes down.*]

Cassius. Come here, sirrah. In Parthia I took you prisoner, and then, when I did not kill you, I made you promise that whatever I told you to do, you would do. Come now, keep your oath. In return you will be a free man. With this good sword that ran through Caesar's body, stab me in the chest. Don't stop to answer me. Here take the handle, cover your face, yes, like that. Stab me. [Pindarus *blindly stabs* Cassius.] Caesar, you are revenged, even with the sword that killed you!

[Cassius *dies.*]

Pindarus. So, I am free. Yet I would not be free if I had dared to do what I wanted. O Cassius, I will run far from this country, where no Roman will see me!

[Pindarus *exits; then* Titinius *and* Messala *enter*.]

Messala. Both sides have victory and defeat, Titinius, for Octavius is beaten by noble Brutus's army, and Cassius's army is beaten by Antony's.

Titinius. This news will comfort Cassius.

Messala. Where did you leave him?

Titinius. He was very upset when I left him. He is with Pindarus, his servant, on this hill.

Messala. Is that Cassius lying on the ground?

Titinius. He isn't moving! O my heart!

Messala. Is that Cassius?

Titinius. No, this *was* Cassius, Messala, but Cassius is no more. O setting sun, as in your red rays you set tonight, so in his red blood Cassius's day is over. The sun of Rome is set. Our day is gone. Clouds, unhealthy rain, and dangers come. Our great works are done. He thought I failed, and killed himself.

Messala. He thought you failed. O hateful error, child of sadness, why do you make men believe things that are not real? O mistake, so quickly born, you always harm the sad mind that gave you birth.

Titinius. Pindarus? Where are you, Pindarus?

Messala. Find him, Titinius. I will go to find the noble Brutus and thrust this news into his ears. I say "thrust," for daggers and poisoned arrows shall be more welcome to Brutus's ears than this news.

Titinius. Go, Messala. I will search for Pindarus.

[Messala *exits.*]

Titinius. Why did you send me out, noble Cassius? I met your friends, and they put this wreath of victory[2] on my head, and told me to give it to you. Did you not hear their joyful shouts? Alas, you misunderstood everything. But, stop. I put this victory wreath on your head. Your Brutus told me to give it to you, and I will do what he asked. Brutus, come quickly and see how good a friend I am to Caius Cassius. With your permission, gods, this is a true Roman's duty! Come Cassius's sword, and find Titinius's heart!

[Titinius *kills himself.*]

[*Trumpets sound.* Brutus, Messala, Young Cato, Strato, Volumnius, *and* Lucilius *enter.*]

---

[2] wreath of victory—a crown of bay tree leaves that Romans put on the head of a winner.

Brutus. Where, where, Messala, is his body?

Messala. Over there, and Titinius mourning over it.

Brutus. Titinius's face is turned upward.

Cato. He is dead!

Brutus. O Julius Caesar, you are mighty yet. Your spirit walks and makes us turn our swords against ourselves.

Cato. Noble Titinius! Look, he has crowned dead Cassius.

Brutus. Are there two Romans living as good as these? Cassius, you were the last of all the Romans, fare you well. Rome will never give birth to your equal. Friends, I owe more tears to this dead man than you shall see me pay. I shall find time, Cassius. I shall find time. Come, let us send his body to Thasos.[3] We will not bury him in camp. It might weaken and sadden the men. Lucilius, come, and come, young Cato, let us go back to the field of battle! Labeo and Flavius, order our armies to fight! It is three o'clock, and, Romans, before night, we shall see how fortune treats us in a second fight.

[*They all exit.*]

---

[3] Thasos—an island near Philippi.

ACT FIVE, SCENE FOUR

In another part of the battlefield, Brutus and his army are in trouble. Lucilius, who pretends to be Brutus, is taken prisoner and brought to Antony. He tells Antony that Brutus will never be taken alive.

[*Trumpets sound. Battle cries are heard.* Brutus, Young Cato, Lucilius, *and others enter.*]

Brutus. Countrymen, keep fighting!

Cato. Only someone who is not a true Roman would stop! Who will go with me? I will attack. They will know my name on the battlefield. [*He shouts*] I am the son of Marcus Cato. An enemy to tyrants and my country's friend! I am the son of Marcus Cato.

[Soldiers *enter and fight.*]

Brutus. And I am Brutus, Marcus Brutus, I! Brutus, my country's friend! Know me for Brutus!

[Brutus *exits fighting.* Young Cato *is killed offstage.*]

Lucilius. O young and noble Cato, have you fallen? Why, now you die as bravely as Titinius and will be honored, being Cato's son.

First Soldier. [*To* Lucilius] **Yield**[1] or die.

Lucilius.[2] I will yield only if you will kill me. [*He offers money.*] Here is money if you will kill me now. Kill Brutus, and be honored in his death.

First Soldier. I must not kill a noble prisoner!

Second Soldier. Stand back! Tell Antony that Brutus has been captured.

First Soldier. I'll tell the news. Here comes the general.

[Antony *enters.*]

First Soldier. Brutus has been captured, my lord!

Antony. Where is he?

---

[1] **Yield**—give up.

[2] Lucilius is pretending to be Brutus.

Lucilius. Safe, Antony. Brutus is safe enough. I dare to tell you that no enemy shall ever take noble Brutus alive. The gods defend him from so great a shame! When you find him, alive or dead, he will be found like Brutus, noble, like himself.

Antony. This is not Brutus, friend, but he is as worthy as Brutus. Keep this man safe. Give him all kindness. I had rather have such men as my friends than my enemies. Go on, and see if Brutus is alive or dead. And bring us word at Octavius's tent how everything has turned out.

[*They all exit.*]

ACT FIVE, SCENE FIVE

In another part of the field, Brutus kills himself to avoid being captured. Antony and Octavius honor Brutus and the battle ends.

[Brutus, Dardanius, Clitus, Strato, *and* Volumnius *enter.*]

Brutus. Come, poor remaining friends, rest on this rock.

Clitus. Statilius signaled we won, but he has not come back, my lord. He has been captured or is dead.

Brutus. [*Aside to* Clitus] Sit down, Clitus. Death is the word. It is in fashion now. Do you understand me, Clitus?[1]

Clitus. What, I , my lord? No, not for all the world.

---

[1] Brutus is suggesting that Clitus kill him.

Brutus. Peace then, don't say anything else about it.

Clitus. I'd rather kill myself.

Brutus. Listen, Dardanius. [*They talk quietly.*]

Dardanius. Could I do such a thing?

Clitus. Dardanius!

Dardanius. Clitus!

Clitus. What terrible question did Brutus ask you?

Dardanius. To kill him, Clitus. Look, he is thinking.

Clitus. Now is Brutus's noble cup overflowing with grief, and it runs over even in his eyes.

Brutus. [*Aside to* Volumnius] Come here, good Volumnius. Listen for a moment.

Volumnius. What do you say, my lord?

Brutus. Why, this, Volumnius, the ghost of Caesar has appeared to me at night two different times, once at Sardis, and last night here at Philippi. I know my hour of death has come.

Volumnius. Not so, my lord.

Brutus. No, I am sure it has come, Volumnius. You see how things are going, Volumnius. Our enemies have beaten us to the edge of death.

[*The bugles are heard sounding attack.*] It's better to leap in ourselves than wait until they push us in. Good Volumnius, we went to school together. Because we have been friends so long, I beg you to hold my sword hilt[2] while I fall on it.

Volumnius. That's not a job for a friend, my lord.

[*More trumpet calls.*]

Clitus. Run, run, my lord, we cannot stay here.

Brutus. [Brutus *shakes each one's hands.*] Farewell to you, and you, and you, Volumnius. Strato, you have been sleeping. Farewell to you too, Strato. Countrymen, my heart is happy that in all my life, I found no man that was not true to me. I shall have more glory this losing day than Octavius and Mark Antony shall gain by winning. So farewell all, for I have almost ended my life's history. Night hangs on my eyes. My bones, which have worked to reach this hour of death, wish to rest now.

[*Battle trumpets.* Soldiers *running and shouting, "Run! Run!"*]

Clitus. Run, my lord, run!

Brutus. Go! I will follow!

---

[2] hilt—handle.

[Clitus, Dardanius, *and* Volumnius *exit.*]

Brutus. I beg you, Strato, stay here with your lord. You are a good fellow with a good reputation. You are an honorable man. Hold my sword, and turn your face away, while I run on it. Will you do this, Strato?

Strato. Give me your hand first. [*They shake hands.*] Fare you well, my lord.

[Strato *holds Brutus's sword and turns his face away.*]

Brutus. Farewell, good Strato—Caesar, now be still! I killed not thee with half so good a will.[3]

[Brutus *runs into the sword blade and dies.*]

[*A trumpet calls retreat.*[4] Octavius, Antony, Messala, Lucilius, *other* Soldiers *enter.*]

Octavius. Who is that?

Messala. My master's servant. Strato, where is your master?

Strato. Not a prisoner as you are, Messala. The conquerors can only make a fire of him,[5] for no one but Brutus conquered Brutus, and no other man gains honor through his death.

---

[3] I kill myself more willingly than I killed you.

[4] retreat—the signal to end the battle.

[5] make a fire of him—cremate Brutus.

Lucilius. It is right we should find Brutus like this! I thank you, Brutus. You have proved my saying true.[6]

Octavius. All that served Brutus, I will take into my service and treat well. Fellow, will you join my service?

Strato. Yes, if Messala will recommend me to you.

Octavius. Do so, good Messala.

Messala. How did Brutus die, Strato?

Strato. I held the sword, and he ran on it.

Messala. Then, Octavius, take him in your service. He was the last to serve his master.

Antony. [*Looking at Brutus's body*] This was the noblest Roman of them all. All the murderers except him did what they did in envy of great Caesar. Brutus only joined the plan to kill Caesar because he thought it was for the good of Rome and her citizens. His life was noble, and the **elements**[7] were so mixed in him that nature might stand up and say to all the world, "This was a man!"

---

[6] In Act Five, Scene Four, Lucilius said, ". . . no enemy shall ever take noble Brutus alive."

[7] **elements**—the pieces out of which all things are made. The Romans thought everything was made of four elements: water, air, earth, and fire.

Octavius. Because he was a good man, let us treat him with respect and give him a proper burial. Place his body in my tent tonight with full military honors. So the battle has ended, let us go to see what glories have been won this happy day.

[*They exit.*]